RECENT PERSPECTIVES
IN
AMERICAN PHILOSOPHY

RECENT PERSPECTIVES
IN AMERICAN PHILOSOPHY

by

YERVANT H. KRIKORIAN

Professor of Philosophy, Emeritus,
The City College of the City University of New York

MARTINUS NIJHOFF - THE HAGUE - 1973

To my esteemed friend
August R. Leisner

ISBN 90 247 1518 0

CONTENTS

PREFACE

The essays in this book analyze significant perspectives of the recent past in American philosophy; they represent some of the major trends of this period. Alfred North Whitehead is included with the recent American philosophers since his major philosophic ideas were fully developed in this country. There has been no attempt to deal comprehensively with this period. Several philosophers of equal importance who also deserve attention—C.I. Lewis, A.O. Lovejoy, W.F. Montague, R.B. Perry, F.J.E. Woodbridge, and others— have not been discussed. Most of the essays were published at various times in various journals. Though all of the perspectives are presented with sympathetic understanding, they are also critically evaluated.

AMERICAN PHILOSOPHY OF THE RECENT PAST

Philosophy at its best is an enlightening reflection on existence and the conscious pursuit of man's maximum good. It is generally an individual enterprise : Plato, Spinoza, and Kant had to do their own solitary philosophic thinking. Yet great social changes, emerging cultural patterns, and new sweeping scientific ideas, by presenting common problems, tend to create philosophic trends.

In a vast dynamic and democratic country like ours where the pace of change is so swift and varied and where men are free to develop alternative conceptions of nature and man there is no official American philosophy. The trends are many, some of native origin, others of foreign importation, and we are too much in the swim of events to appraise them as objectively as we should like.

Looking over the various prevalent doctrines in the country one discerns a large variety of philosophies, yet it remains true that the recent and current trend in American philosophy has its own distinctive identity. The major trend in recent American philosophy can be characterized as empiricism in the broad sense of this term, an empiricism that is blended with experimentalism, functionalism, and temporalism. Given this broad meaning of empiricism, it may be said that whereas continental philosophy is existential and British philosophy is analytical, American philosophy is empirical.

The empirical temper in philosophy, of course, is not something that belongs exclusively to America; it has a long history, stemming mainly from the English empiricists of the 17th century. In American philosophy Chauncey Wright, C.S. Peirce, and William James and, more recently, John Dewey and Edgar A. Singer, Jr. are some of the most important exponents of empiricism. Early in the century the pragmatic and the realistic schools, and in the thirties the logical empiricists and the phenomenologists contributed to the empirical temper.

But even more than individual philosophers and schools of philosophy the larger background of contemporary American life has nourished the empirical spirit. Science as the most pervasive climate of our intellectual and practical activity has enhanced the empirical attitude. The great development, in this country, of business and technological industry has encouraged the pragmatic, empirical outlook.

Empiricism, however, is an ambiguous term, and its different meanings have different philosophic consequences. For some it means that only concrete personal experience can be accepted as reality; for others it means the succession of sense-impressions. The more recent usage, the one that has been dominant in American philosophy, identifies empiricism with objectively and socially verifiable pronouncements, that is, with experimentalism, or confirmation through demonstrable evidence.

Modern empiricism or experimentalism is not opposed to reason. Traditionally empiricism and rationalism have been in philosophic conflict with each other. The empiricism that is dominant in recent American philosophy is fully aware of the significance of reason or of logical order in science. There are, of course, many controversial issues here. For some, like Morris Cohen, reason has ontological status, but for many others its role is functional and operational in the pursuit of knowledge. Thinking, from the latter point of view, is not staring at a ready-made world, but is a creative process in the solution of problems. Ideas are projects of action, anticipatory actions that remain to be fulfilled.

The experimental method has not only technical but great human significance. To win different realms of existence for objectivity, for the kind of truth that anyone can verify through experience, is indeed, as one American philosopher has said, "a brave adventure, and whether they meet victory or defeat one cannot refuse one's enthusiasm to those who have had the courage to make it".[1]

The bearing of the empirical temper on recent contemporary theories of value or ethics in America also deserves consideration.

For the empiricists and functionalists all values have their abode in the natural world, either in actualities to be enjoyed or as possibilities to be hoped for. First came the emphasis on biological evolution

---

[1] E.A. Singer, Jr., *Modern Thinkers and Present Problems* (New York : Macmillan Co., 1929), p. 32.

in relation to value, a theory that established continuity between the animal world and the human world. Then came the psychological, behavioristic approach to value. R.B. Perry's notion that "a thing has value when it is an object of interest", and Dewey's greater emphasis on the place of intelligence in value experience have been very influential on theories of value. More recently American philosophers have been explaining in considerable detail the notion of value in the social, cultural, and semantic spheres. All these approaches have fruitfully employed the empirical procedure.

Important consequences follow from this approach to value. First of all, greater respect is given to natural, concrete human experience and its potentialities. Empirical theories of value emphasize the pursuit of values that are open to us in our natural world. Another important consequence is that the only effective way to regulate values is through critical, intelligent, pragmatic appraisal. To promote the maximum welfare of this country we need not accept docilely the allegedly absolute values that some groups would thrust upon us; what we must do is to reappraise pragmatically all of our values.

The kind of philosophy under discussion also presents a generalized outlook on existence.

The empirical outlook has been one of the major forces in the vigorous development of naturalism by John Dewey, F.J.E. Woudbridge, R. Sellars, and others. In recent years some of the leading American philosophers have further developed naturalism. And other types of philosophy—the idealistic, the personalistic, and the theistic—have also been deeply influenced by the empirical temper and to a degree have made basic modifications in their assumptions.

The empirical temper has also led to a pluralistic view of the world. Reality is conceived with all its discontinuities and loose connections, rather than as a completely integrated system where all relations are internal and form a network of unbroken implications. That reality is in one sense a whole may be admitted, but the issue is, in what sense is it a whole? Nature or reality may be a whole as an integrated, logical system; or it may be a whole, as William James argues, "... diffused and distributed, in the form of an indefinitely, numerous lot of *eaches*, coherent in all sorts of ways and degrees".[2] Though events are related in many different ways, they are not all related in a logical, necessitarian way. There are internal relations as well as

---

[2] *Pragmatism*, (New York : Longman, Green & Co., 1913), p. 264.

external relations. There are thus novelties, contingencies, genuine alternative possibilities.

This empirical philosophic outlook is also non-reductive in its interpretation of nature. This is especially true of the recent naturalistic philosophy in America. Unlike the traditional materialistic theories of the "nothing but" attitude, events are taken to be part of nature with all their qualitative differences. Although living and mental beings may be physical at every point, from the organization of physical entities non-physical qualities may emerge which are as genuine aspects of nature as the physical. To speak of adaptation, survival, thinking, wishing, and hoping in purely physical terms does not convey the actual meaning of these activities. What is important is the contextual interpretation of events. If in the grouping of physical elements new properties emerge, then these properties can be classified as their nature demands. The logician, especially the modern logician, is conversant with the fact that the same object may be put into different classes, depending on the property that is being focused upon.

Finally, the empirical temper of thought finds its full expression in temporalism or process philosophy. The beginning of process philosophy belongs to the past, especially to the eighteenth century, but its maturity has been reached in the twentieth century. Its most vigorous development has been in America. The leading exponents of this philosophy have been the following : S. Alexander and H. Bergson abroad, and in this country William James, John Dewey, George Mead, Alfred Whitehead, and Roy Sellars. Process metaphysics is not a rigidly doctrinaire system. Among its adherents are idealists, materialists, theists, and naturalists. Nor is it confined to professional philosophers, since many scientists, artists, men of affairs, and religious leaders have been influenced by it.

In many respects process philosophy expresses the American spirit. Its keynote is progress. Change is universal, and change is creative and cumulative. The past is not discarded, but transformed into something new. As Whitehead, one of the major exponents of this philosophy, has said, "The ultimate metaphysical principle is the advance from disjunction to conjunction, creating a novel entity other than the entities given in disjunction".[3] And for Dewey, whose major concern is with the human situation, "growing, or

---

[3] *Process and Reality*, (New York : Macmillan Co., (1929), p. 32.

continuous reconstruction of experience is the only end" to life.[4]
This progress is from the lower to the higher, an upward emergence
in nature rather than a downward emanation from God. For most
process philosophers nature is of one piece, with no support from the
supernatural. The purview of process and progress is of this world.

The process philosophy is a forward-looking one, centered upon
possibilities. The emphasis is on adventure, on new ways of living,
on new social institutions, on new civilizations. Its motive for progress
is not merely release from misery, but the love of change, of novelty,
of abundance. In process philosophy the lure of ideal possibilities
is the dominant theme. Even "god" is defined as the union of all ideal
possibilities arousing men to action. For the Thomist, being is good,
for the process philosopher, becoming is good.

On the whole, most of the recent American philosophers, especially
the important ones, have regarded their philosophic systems as tentative or provisional. Philosophic constructions, like scientific ones,
are inherently incomplete or lacking in finality. Peirce had earlier
given expression to this spirit in his idea of fallibilism : "Fallibilism
is the doctrine that our knowledge is never absolute but always swims,
as it were, in the continuum of uncertainty and indeterminacy".

For this attitude of recent philosophers there are several reasons :
the limitations of experience, defective insight, and the obscurities
of language. Recently philosophers have become especially aware
of the treacheries involved in language. And, in some cases, as in process
philosophy, the very nature of the philosophic formulations is always
bound to be incomplete.

Recent American philosophy has been a vigorous and many-sided
activity. No system has had a monopoly; each added its own insight.
It has been analytic, eager to clarify ideas, but, above all, it has been
intensely and dominantly empirical, fruitfully applying this attitude
to many areas of thought. Despite the variety of metaphysical commitments and theories of value, there has been basic agreement on
the desirability of focusing on practical and humanistic ideals.

What can the future expect? That will depend partly on whether
the philosophy we create will be vitally relevant to our civilization,
and partly on whether the type of civilization we create will be conducive to philosophic growth.

---

[4] *John Dewey's Philosophy*, Edited by J. Ratner (New York : Modern Library,
1939), p. 628.

II

DEWEY AND THE ETHICS OF NATURALISM

In the last hundred years or so, great changes have taken place in our conception of the physical world, of man and society, as well as in our pattern of living. The theory of organic evolution, by establishing continuity between man and other living beings, has shown him to be a product of nature. Social and cultural researches, by uncovering a large variety of culture patterns, have given a clearer account of the structure of society. At the turn of the century, relativity and quantum theories provided us with a new picture of nature. Equally striking have been the changes in our mode of living. Technology and industrialization have imposed new shapes on our civilization. There has been an intense urbanization, and a consequent change in community and family life.

John Dewey, who was born in the year Darwin's *Origin of Species* was first published, passed through all these changes, and his philosophy was shaped by the demands and conflicts that resulted from them. Philosophy, if it is to be significant in a culture, has to deal with the important issues of that culture. The major conflict that characterizes our civilization, as Dewey has persistently maintained, is between the growing power of science and technology on the one hand and the lagging moral attitudes and social institutions on the other. Traditional morality, with its pre-scientific attitude, is still a pervasive factor, but it is out of harmony with the demands of contemporary life. Science has established continuity between man and nature, but the older morality is still based on extra-natural sanctions. Science insists on observation and experiment to solve our problems, but the older morality demands fixed standards or imperatives. Technology and industry have rendered obsolete institutions to which the older morality still clings. There is a sharp dualism within our civilization: how shall we resolve it?

Dewey deals boldly with this cleavage between science and traditional morality. His central thesis is that it must be overcome by naturalizing ethics—by placing man in nature, by determining moral values and standards in terms of human experience, and, above all, by using the experimental method in dealing with ethical problems. To naturalize ethics is to change it into an empirical enterprise. But this process does not mean for Dewey, as is sometimes believed, that the ideal aspects of life should be disregarded or belittled; what it does mean is that continuity must be established between them and the natural conditions of life.

Dewey's naturalistic ethics, in its broad outline, is clear and impressive, but many of its details are open to controversy. His analysis is not always easy to follow and some of his arguments are involved and seamless. But for the present we should not be diverted from the broad aspects of his ethics, which constitute a major philosophic contribution to our era.

Ethics is concerned with human conduct. On the whole, this concern has two aspects, or differences in emphasis. One of them has been the formulation of rules or imperatives to check desires or impulses. In this sense, ethics is primarily a matter of what one should not do or of what negative commandments one should obey. Yet in its positive sense ethics is less interested in such prohibitions than in discovering and realizing ends or values, the object being to make of life a worthwhile experience. Dewey has always emphasized this positive aspect. As far back as his *The Study of Ethics : A Syllabus*, written in 1894, he expressed his conviction that amid the prevalence of "pathological and moralistic ethics, there is room for a theory which conceives of conduct as the normal and free living of life as it is". From this standpoint the task of ethics resolves itself into one major inquiry—the search for the nature of human good. Dewey's ethics in this positive sense involves many important ideas. I shall consider some of the more distinctive ones.

First, if ethics is concerned with good, we should try to understand what Dewey means by the term good, or rather by the term value, the latter being more commonly used in contemporary philosophic discussions. Value is a central idea in ethics. Such terms as "good and bad", "right and wrong", "justice ane injustice", and "the highest good" involve the notion of value. Some find the source and meaning of value, especially when the adjective "higher" is added, in some extra-empirical realm or notion, like divine authority or an a priori absolute;

others find the source and meaning of value in natural, human experience. Dewey's view of value is of the latter kind.

Usually those who claim that the source and meaning of value reside in human experience identify it with desire or interest. "Value consists", writes a contemporary philosopher, "in the fulfillment of an interest as such"; and by interest is meant "a subject's liking or disliking". Cigarettes have value for those who like smoking; music for the lovers of music; power for ambitious men. This view has been effectively defended by Santayana, Russell, and especially by Perry, whose words I have just quoted.

To a certain extent Dewey agrees with this standpoint, since it connects values with concrete human experiences and satisfactions, and thus avoids the pallid remoteness of purely rationalistic or non-empirical approaches. Yet he finds the formulation limited and inadequate. For Dewey, if desire is to yield a meaningful notion of value, one must introduce a judgment, a comparison, or an appraisal. What he is insisting upon may be illustrated by the difference between desire and the desirable, between satisfaction and the satisfactory, between liking and the likable. In the second member of each pair the notion of estimation, criticism, appraisal is involved, so that desire or liking had acquired new properties.

Valuation, from this standpoint, is concerned with the means-consequence relation. In this sense medicine is good for the patient, and a car for one who intends to travel. Moreover, valuation as appraisal is a prescription, not merely a description, of fact. When a doctor tells a patient that a certain way of living is good for his recovery, he is not merely stating a fact but giving a rule, which the patient must follow to regain his health. Finally, and this is important for Dewey, appraisals and judgments of value are open to empirical verification. The doctor's prescription is not something purely personal; it is based on the facts of the situation.

If value is what is appraised, the transition to ethical value is a natural and an important one. Many values are amoral. When one says this pen is good, this musical piece is pleasant, a summer vacation on the seashore is better than one in the mountains, one has no moral questions in mind. Morality deals only with certain types of values, those designated by "right" or "wrong". What is the meaning of these ethical terms?

Dewey's analysis of ethical value is not as incisive as his notion of value in general. In reading some of his writings one gets the impression that there is no difference between value judgment and ethical judgment. Yet when Dewey's ethics is considered in its broader setting, he does make a distinction. Whenever "alternative possibilities" or "better-or-worse" qualities have important social, human consequences, they attain moral quality. He sees the distinction between value and ethical value as a matter of degree—of the importance of alternative actions to human, social interrelations—rather than a matter of difference in kind. In this sense, as Dewey rightly argues, any act may attain moral quality. Walking in itself is a trivial, amoral event, but if it involves going at some risk to another's aid, it may take on a moral meaning.

More precisely stated, morality is concerned with conflicting desires which "promise opposed goods" and "incompatible courses of action" in relation to their effect upon human interests and social relationships. The consequences involved in "incompatible courses of action" may be rather limited, as when the use of one's money is concerned; or they may be of worldwide importance, as when the use of the atomic bomb is concerned. The task of morality is to examine critically the consequences of alternative actions, to appraise them, in some cases to suggest a new alternative action, and finally to resolve the conflict through thought in such a way that the result will be beneficial to both the individual and society. Morally this result will be the right one, the one that ought to be. And "thought" here should not be taken in the rationalistic sense of apprehending certain non-empirical moral truths, but in the experimental sense of finding ways and means to solve the given problem.

Another important aspect of Dewey's ethics is his treatment of moral standards or ideals. The traditional moralist finds his standards already fashioned for him and sanctioned under such pretentious titles as "the moral law", "the moral order", "the wisdom of the Fathers". These absolutes are to be regarded less as means of solving behavior problems than as symbols to revere, to be loyal to. Moral experience, as Dewey sees it, is not movement toward some well-defined and fixed goal which authority or reason can formulate in the form of universal maxims or categorical imperatives; rather it continually feels its way toward fresh sources of insight in order to exploit the potentialities of life. In this process, moral standards should be regarded as hypotheses to be verified by experience, as instruments to guide us in our attempt to keep pace with expanding knowledge and opportunities.

Dewey has been frequently criticized for the relativistic implications of his ethics; and some of his sayings might justifiably provoke such criticism. But what he is primarily concerned wiht is that moral ideals should be allowed to grow and not be frozen into fixed authoritarian rigidity. Even such a fruitful ideal as liberty, unless modified in its meaning and application in relation to concrete circumstances, may cease to be an agent in the beneficial shaping of experience.

Nevertheless, Dewey's ethics does contain a near-absolute standard for conduct. It is growth, growth of the individual and especially of society. "Growth itself", he writes, "is the only moral 'end' ".[1] He pitches aspiration high : "Nothing but the best, the richest and fullest experience possible, is good enough for man".[2] Growth or progress thus means increase of rich meanings, especially in present experience, and this increase is in all dimensions—finer sensory distinctions, harmony, and unification. Therefore Dewey's categorical imperative is this : "So act as to increase the meaning of present experience".[3] Ultimately, it is in terms of this imperative that acts have to be determined as good or bad, right or wrong. A major consequence of the identification of moral ideals with growth is the need to supplement the narrow, self-centered individualism of the past with a new social conception of individuality, an individuality consonant with the industrial conditions under which we live.

But even this inclusive ideal of growth should not be mistaken for a fixed absolute and thus be changed to a sterile standard. To achieve the more richly informed concrete qualities of experience one should steer clear of abstractions and carefully study the specific needs and alternative possibilities within a localized situation. "Till men give up the search for a general formula of progress they will not know where to look to find it".[4]

There is a final question to be considered. How will human good and satisfaction be realized? Here we come to Dewey's idea of the relation of means to ends in ethics. Dewey has tirelessly insisted on the importance of this relation. He is eager to make ideal possibilities actualities, and the method he suggests is the determination of the true relation between means and ends.

---

[1] *Reconstruction in Philosophy* (New York : Henry Holt & Co., 1926), p. 177.
[2] *Experience and Nature* (Chicago, London, Open Court Pub. Co., 1925), p. 412.
[3] *Human Nature and Conduct* (New York : Henry Holt Co., 1922), p. 283.
[4] *Ibid.*, p. 283.

For Dewey, means and ends form a continuum. Ends—or, better, ends-in-view are the construction of a series of means. Apart from means, ends have no basis. Anyone genuinely interested in an end, such as becoming a musician, must be affectionately concerned with the means of achieving this end—that is, with a knowledge of musical pieces and instruments and with the requisite techniques. Moreover, in the continuum of means and ends, means are ends for the time being, and ends are means for new ends-in-view. The relation of means to ends is a continuous process in life; the distinction between them is purely relative.

The final character of an accomplished moral act depends on the character of the means used; the end is really the summation of the series of means. A democratic ideal cannot be attained by non- or anti-democratic means, since the democratic way of life is means and end in their continuous interrelation. A moral society cannot be constructed on the basis of immoral means. Thus morality applies to means as well as to ends, to the various parts of our activity as well as to the activity as a whole.

Moreover, if means and ends are internally related, then the reconstruction of morals must lean heavily on the sciences, especially on the social sciences. Intelligent formulation of morals in sex, business, politics and international relations depends heavily on the specific empirical facts in these areas. Without these facts and their use, morals in such fields are sentimental. The sharp separation between means and ends, between material conditions and ideal ends, between science and morals, must cease. Apart from material conditions, ideals are merely ineffective aspirations; apart from ideal ends, material activities tend to become narrow and harsh.

The central theme that runs through Dewey's analysis of means and ends and through all his ethical discussion, is the belief that intelligence expressed through the experimental method should be applied to moral problems and conflicts. Whether this method will succeed where the traditional methods of authoritarianism and absolutism have failed is itself an experimental question, but it is an adventure supremely worth undertaking.

Dewey's ethical system forms a coherent, comprehensive and vitally effective whole based on the facts of life and the possibilities of experience; yet htis ethics may be enlarged in certain directions within the framework of his experimental philosophy.

It should be noted that, despite his thoroughgoing empiricism,

Dewey has not given sufficient consideration to the empirical question of the content of moral ideals. Pragmatically it is of great importance to enrich the content of desirable moral ends, since the richer they are the more effective they will be in conduct. What type of individual life, family relations, economic and political institutions is most desirable, not only in terms of general principles but in a more or less detailed form? A naturalistic ethics, if it is to be a genuine alternative to the traditional systems, cannot ignore this phase of morality. The suggestion is not to reinstate what Dewey rightly decries—the authoritative setting up of ideals for conduct prior to experience. What is being maintained is that certain large, desirable ends may be tentatively formulated and evaluated before dealing with specific situations. It is not enough to know how to do things; it is equally important to have some idea of what we want to do. The relatively concrete content of ideals must therefore become the concern of ethics. Of course, as Dewey maintains, the ideal ends should be plastic and progressively defined in terms of the conflicts and obstacles involved and of the means that are available.

Moreover, Dewey has not troubled himself to show the application of intelligence to a certain area of experience—the tragic, hopeless, insoluble predicaments of life. Dewey is so passionately concerned with the possible growth of human life that he has neglected to comment on the significance of resignation and equanimity. These, too, are the fruits of intelligence. Dewey's moral attitude is not unlike that expressed in Spinoza's famous saying : "A free man thinks of nothing less than of death, and his wisdom is not meditation upon death but upon life". It is true that the energy we have should be spent more for the enhancement of life than for the discipline of facing defeat; yet the philosophy of human conduct is not complete until it acknowledges the darker aspects of life and indicates attitudes that are relevant to them.

The suggestions made here both as to the pragmatic preliminary enrichment of ideal content and of the constructive role of resignation or equanimity in a dominantly active life can be incorporated into the body of Dewey's ethics. The very fact that his ethics can thus be further developed is a sign of its intrinsic fertility.

In its fundamentals Dewey's ethical theory is one of the most vital and relevant philosophies of conduct in contemporary thought. Grounded in human experience and natural events, it is an ethics exhilaratingly free from extra-empirical or super-naturalistic dogmas.

Insisting on the application of experimental method or creative intelligence, it is an ethics as much opposed to the policy of listless drifting as to every kind of harsh authoritarianism. Finally, it is an ethics that is not satisfied with what is barely good enough for human beings but demands the richest possible experience of which they are capable.

III

COHEN'S RATIONALISTIC NATURALISM

Morris Raphael Cohen was one of the most eminent figures in recent American philosophy. His critical mind, his erudition, his incisive expression, and his philosophic outlook made him a unique figure. His major work is *Reason and Nature*. Some of his other important books are *The Meaning of History*, *Law and the Social Order* and *Preface to Logic*. Cohen had a deep interest in the philosophy of science, in metaphysics, in social philosophy, in legal philosophy, and in the philosophy of history. His contribution to legal philosophy especially has been widely recognized. The present discussion of his philosophy will be limited to his general view of nature with some reference to his ethical theory.

I

Cohen's general outlook is naturalistic, for there is no place in his philosophy for the supernatural, and no place for extra-scientific methods to attain reliable knowledge. His outlook is also rationalistic, for rationality is assumed to be inherent in nature. His rationalistic naturalism is based upon three principles : the principle of rationality, the principle of invariance, and the principle of polarity. These three principles, coherently interwoven, give rise to an impressive view of reality.

1. Rationality : The concept of rationality has had a long history, and it has acquired a variety of meanings. It has meant logical order, inductive generalization, and wisdom. Each of these meanings has been significant. Cohen does not offer an inclusive definition of rationality, such as would be applicable to all cases. In his philosophy of nature the first is dominant, and in his ethical theory the third is central.

Rationality as logical order may be considered methodologically or ontologically. Methodologically it is a procedure to order our objects of thought in a logical way. Most philosophers, with the exception of mystics and irrationalists, feel the necessity of such a procedure. For many there is no controversial issue here. Yet Cohen goes beyond the methodological use of rationality and insists on its ontological status. Rational order for Cohen is actually inherent in nature. The rules of logic and pure mathematics for Cohen "may be viewed not only as principles of inference applicable to all systems but also as descriptive of certain abstract invariant relations which constitute an objective order characteristic of any subject matter".[1]

As against idealists, positivists, and pragmatists, he is firm in insisting that the rational order is independent of the human or the super-human mind. Idealists, according to Cohen, deny the objectivity of logical order by giving it only a psychological status; but the psychological description of reasoning as a mental event cannot determine, according to Cohen, whether a given logical argument is valid. Positivists, the arch philosophic enemies of Cohen, fall short in a similar way. As sensations are taken to be the only deliverances of the external world, logical connections are regarded as mere fictions. Pragmatists similarly, Cohen argues, depreciate the status of rational order. In their attempt to interpret the truth of judgment in terms of practical consequences, they consider logical relations merely as practical tools of thought with no ontological standing.

Cohen, of course, is not a fanatical rationalist trying to reduce everything to reason. He admits an element of contingency in nature. "By no amount of reasoning", he writes, "can we altogether eliminate all contingency from our world".[2] And again : "Rationality does not exhaust existence. The relational form of pattern points to a non-rational or alogical element without which the former has no genuine meaning".[3] Ultimately the universe is what it is and contingency is uneliminable. Yet we should bear in mind that it is rationality that gives objective essence to objects, which our mental activity, if fortunate, is capable of discovering.

If mind can discover the rationality that is inherent in nature, what then is the structure of mind, and what is the relation of mind

---

[1] *Reason and Nature* (New York : Harcourt Brace & Co., 1931), p. 143.
[2] *Ibid.*, p. 82.
[3] *Ibid.*, p. 164.

to nature? Cohen has not developed any detailed theory of mind. His view of mind is on the whole in the realistic tradition. Mind is characterized by consciousness, awareness. Intellectual activity, creativity, and affective and volitional behavior are attributed to mind. But on the issue in question, whether mind contributes anything to our knowledge of the rationality of nature, Cohen maintains that mind is in no sense a contributor but merely a discoverer of the logical order.

2. Invariance : The general notion of rationality is further developed by the principle of invariance. This principle is discussed in the context of scientific method.

Science is not, as Cohen rightly points out, a mere observation of particular facts; it is never satisfied with stating only what has occurred. The aim of science is to determine the universal, invariant relations of paritcular events. To say that sulphur has melted at 125° C. is a mere statement of fact similar to the statement that Russians for generations have used the Cyrillic alphabet; but to say that sulphur always melts at 125° C means that if ever anything conforms to the category of sulphur it melts at this temperature. The last statement expresses not only a historical event but an invariant relation which belongs to "the eternal present".[4]

We must make a distinction, Cohen says, between the nature of anything and its manifestations. Science, as earlier mentioned, is not satisfied with mere description of particular events; it seeks the reasons why particular events occur in the way they do. To the question why certain events occur, science answers by giving the reason, by putting the events into a system so that, "knowing the nature of the system and certain data ..., we can deduce or form a rational account of the events to be explained".[5] In this procedure the abstract laws that make intelligible the concrete, particular facts should not be considered as being less real than the events that are explained.

Cohen draws a similar distinction between change and constancy. Modern thought emphasizes change, mobility, and flux, but the claim that only change is real is, for Cohen, a "snap judgment resting on no proof of logic or fact".[6] Change is undoubtedly a universal aspect of existence, but so, for Cohen, is constancy. If the growth of science

---

[4] *Ibid.*, pp. 99-101.
[5] *Ibid.*, p. 157.
[6] *Ibid.*, p. 18.

has dissolved the eternity of the hills or the fixity of the species, it has also established new constancies for many seemingly chaotic events. Changes can have no definite characters, Cohen argues, without patterns that are identical. To argue that constant rules of logic cannot be true of a world of flux is a "confusion as gross as to argue that motion cannot have constant velocity or a fixed direction".[7]

Though the essence of particular things is their invariant relations, our knowledge of these is only probable. Only in logic or in mathematics can we attain certainty; in the world of facts our knowledge is only probable, for we cannot prove that the contrary of a given factual statement is absolutely impossible. Even the best established statements of science, such as Newton's laws of motion or the law of conservation of energy, which undoubtedly offer the best explanation to hosts of phenomena, are not absolutely certain; it is always possible that we may find phenomena that do not conform to these statements and that other hypotheses may explain them better.[8] Though our knowledge of empirical facts is always probable and subject to error, yet it is open to self-correction. There is, therefore, progress in science. Yet this self-corrective process is always within the system of science itself, and not in some extranatural system.

One other point must be mentioned. Cohen strongly emphasizes the dependence of scientific method on the principle of causality. This principle, in turn depends on the larger principle of sufficient reason, which is formulated as follows : "Everything is connected in definite ways with definite other things, so that its full nature is not revealed except by its position and relations within a system".[9] This principle does not imply that the whole universe must be taken as the cause of any of the particular facts; the cause ascribed to anything must be something determinate. Cohen attacks "vicious organicism" which attempts, à la Hegel, to make knowledge of everything the presupposition of knowledge of anything.

Yet in Cohen's philosophy there is a place for the idea of the universe as a whole. We need such an idea to characterize the incompleteness and fragmentariness of our actual knowledge. And in knowing the meaning of any fragment as a fragment "we know the direction of

---

[7] *Ibid.*, p. 19.

[8] *Ibid.*, p. 126, also *A Preface to Logic* (New York : Henry Holt & Co., 1924), p, 100.

[9] *Reason and Nature*, p. 150.

completion".[10] In this sense Cohen finds no objection to the assertion that a knowledge of the absolute is involved in any true knowledge of phenomena. Eternity thus becomes a limit or ordering principle of a series of expanding vistas. For Cohen such a limit is an ideal, but an ideal that should not be dismissed as merely mental. It is "a genuine condition of the series of stages in the self-corrective system of natural science".[11]

3. Polarity : The third principle to be examined is the principle of polarity. According to this principle opposites involve each other. As Cohen expresses it, "... opposites such as immediacy and mediation, unity and plurality, the fixed and the flux, substance and function, ideal and real, actual and possible, etc., like the north (positive) and the south (negative) poles of a magnet, all involve each other when applied to any significant entity".[12]

For Cohen the principle of polarity is first of all "a maxim of intellectual search"; it helps us to clarify vagueness of expression and to interrelate opposite demands. In discussing general categories of existence like unity and plurality, fixity and flux, or social categories like individuality and collectivity, or moral categories like individuality and collectivity, or moral categories like absolutism and relativism of standards, the principle of polarity guides our thinking to more adequate insights by showing the necessity and the fruitfulness of these opposites.

There are also apparently contradictory and incompatible views which may be harmonized by analysis that is akin to polar analysis. Take as illustration the statement that a house is thirty years old and that it is thirty-one years old. Logically these two statements are contradictory; yet if we draw the necessary distinctions and say that it is thirty-one years old from the beginning of the building of the house, but thirty years old from its completion, the two contradictory statements are true. And, again, the statements that X is generous and that he is not generous are incompatible, but if we learn that X is generous to his family, but ungenerous to his employees, the truth of the two statements becomes possible. Statements taken abstractly may be incompatible, but if the same statements are applied to concrete existences, and also assigned to their proper separate domains, they may be compatible.

[10] *Ibid.*, p. 156.
[11] *Ibid.*, p. 156.
[12] *Ibid.*, p. 165.

The principle of polarity may have methodological use for the clarification of ideas, but for Cohen it stands for something more. For him, the principle of polarity, like the principle of rationality, has ontological status. Empirical facts are said to be resultants of opposing tendencies like the north and south poles. Cohen generalizes this alleged fact as the principle of "the necessary copresence and mutual dependence of opposite determinations".[13] Thus the principle of polarity is not only a procedural guide but also an objective phase of reality.

Cohen applies his principle of polarity to major metaphysical issues. Many of the philosophic conflicts result, he thinks, from the fact that the adherents of different views uncritically accept one alternative without recognizing the degree of truth in other views. Cohen agrees with Leibnitz that great philosophers are generally right in what they assert (of their own vision) and wrong in what they deny (of the vision of others).[14] If unity and plurality, substance and function, ideal and real are opposites, then any metaphysics that disregards either would be partial. Somehow for an adequate philosophy opposites must be taken into account.

4. Ethics : So far the major principles of Cohen's metaphysics have been stated and their significance shown in his philosophy of nature. The bearing of these principles on his theory of ethics will now be indicated.

Can science be applied to the art of living? This is the question which concerns Cohen in his discussion of ethics. There are some obvious difficulties in this pursuit. Because moral judgments are deeply rooted in the customs of our society, it is difficult to uproot ourselves from these customs and to question their truth. Another difficulty is that a scientific ethics may be misinterpreted by the unintelligent with harmful results. These and other conditions tend to make moral discussion a mere apologetics for the existing customs and institutions. Yet despite these difficulties the moral philosopher must approach his task with critical spirit and the ethical neutrality of the scientist.

Historically there have been two major and opposite theories of morality—the absolutistic and the relativistic. For the absolutist moral rules are absolute, eternally binding. Moral laws are not made

[13] *A Preface to Logic*, p. 75.
[14] *Studies in Philosophy and Science* (New York : F. Unger Publishing Co.‘ 1944), p. 13.

by man but imposed by God or some other supreme power. For the relativist there are no fixed universal standards of morality : moral precepts depend on individuals and groups. Sumner, one of the pioners of cultural relativism, argues that mores can make anything right. Cohen examines both of these theories and finds them unsatisfactory. The absolutist is too rigid and uncritical, the relativist is too chaotic, without guiding principles. Cohen thinks the principle of polarity can reconcile the two opposing views. These two views actually provide a vantage point for arriving at the truth. Concretely every issue of life involves choice. The absolutist is right "in insisting that every such choice logically involves a principle of decision", and the relativist is right "in insisting on the primacy of the feeling or perception of the demands in the actual case before us".[15] We may thus have an ethical system that is rigorously logical and at the same time richly empirical. Such an ethics must be grounded in what human beings desire and believe, and yet its primary condition must be the logical analysis of judgment as to what constitutes right and wrong, good and evil, and so become the rational formulation of our ends.

Cohen does not offer any detailed account of what these ends should be. As a naturalist he points out that the rational ends of conduct are not outside human activity itself, but are inherent in life. Yet though the ends to be pursued are not transcendental, they should not be too narrowly conceived. Hedonism has its place, but hedonism tends to conceive morality too much in terms of prudence. Calculation is more readily applied to the tangible and more obvious phases of life. One should not ignore those finer or larger virtues that heighten the significance of life. The rational life must keep a place for heroic actions and for the pursuit of unattainable ideals.

The universe that has emerged from Cohen's analysis may be summarized as follows. The universe is a rational system; yet it is a pluralistic universe with the uneliminable element of contingency. Polarity is a pervasive of reality, and thus the empirical world is one where opposites involve each other. The road to knowledge is through science, or the discovery of the invariant relations between particular events. The universe is intelligible in its own terms, without introducing explanatory principles from without. Man's place in this world is episodic; yet life should be guided by rational ideals.

[15] *Reason and Nature*, p. 438.

II

Cohen presents a challenging view of the universe. His emphasis on reason, polarity and rational conduct is rich with meaning. Yet there are certain points in his philosophy that are open to question.

Cohen's rationalistic realism, the theory that rationality is an objective trait of nature, fails to make clear the distinction between the functional role of reason in science and the ontological assertions about it. This lack of clear distinction is a source of ambiguity throughout his discussions. He criticizes philosophers like Mach, Dewey, and others, insisting that they do not understand the nature of science, but his criticisms are misplaced, for the philosophers he criticizes are fully aware of the importance of abstractions, universals, invariant relations, laws, in a word, of reason in science, except that they do not entertain his ontological view of reason. It will be necessary to distinguish between the methodological and the metaphysical issues involved.

The philosophic issue that Cohen's view of rationality raises is the following : Does the central importance of reason in science necessarily involve Cohen's rationalistic realism? Does the scientist merely describe an objective, rational order of nature without contributing any element to this order? Affirmative answers to these questions seem to be unwarranted. Cohen's ontological view of reason is extraneous to the operational function of reason in science.

Nature is the object of scientific knowledge, but this knowledge is not obtained by a passive acceptance of facts. Scientific explanation always involves stipulations, specified conditions, laws under which the determination of events holds. Cohen himself insists on this point. To give meaning, for example, to the statement that a body moves one must know its velocity under the stipulated conditions. There is thus a distinction between so-called observable facts and the stipulations and classifications to which they are subjected by the mind. So-called facts may be independent of some classification, but not of all classification. Even the facts to be classified are resultants of prior classifications. Cohen is certainly aware of all this, but he is unwilling to admit that the creative activity of mind involves any element of free choice, or contributes any element to the rational order of nature. Yet the examination of the operational functioning of science shows that the scientist has a certain degree of choice in his theories and is thus a contributor to the order of nature. Operationally scientific theories are not mere descriptions, but creative inventions not unlike inventions of technical instruments.

The Copernical picture of the solar system as against the Ptolemaic was the result of creative imagination and of choice. This choice was not based on new observation; it was a choice between two images that were analytically connected, Copernicus deciding to pass from one to the other by specific transformation. Similarly Newton's great achievement was the result of imagination and choice. His choice was between a great number of possible laws falling within the probable error of his data. Newton, basing his thought on the separate inductions of Galileo and Kepler, was able to formulate a single law that was close to, but not identical with, them.

In a sense scientific theories are "arbitrary". This does not mean that they are capricious, but only that they result from a choice that is guided by the ideals of science, such as simplicity, comprehensiveness, and pragmatic productivity.

There are also debatable issues in Cohen's principle of polarity. For Cohen the principle of polarity is a "maxim of intellectual search" as well as a "necessary copresence and mutual dependence of opposite determinations". As a maxim of intellectual search this principle has many points in its favor : it leads one to a larger philosophic orientation, it helps one to reconcile many apparent contradictions, it enables one to do justice to many conflicting vital demands. Cohen has used it effectively, and has developed through it a comprehensive philosophic system. And yet this principle has serious limitations; we cannot decide troublesome issues by it in the manner Cohen suggests. In our thinking we all like to do justice to categories like unity and plurality, fixity and flux, causality and purpose, mind and body, nature and supernature. Even if we all use the principle of polarity, the factual conditions, our deep personal motives, or our general philosophic outlook will give a different twist to our judgments. Each philosopher will claim to allocate a place to opposite categories but in each the place will be different. For the monist there is a place for plurality, but only as a phase of an organic whole; for the nominalist there is a place for the universal, yet quite different from that of the Platonic idealist; for the naturalist there is a place for the supernatural, but only in the realm of imagination. How can the principle of polarity settle such issues? Does Cohen mean, what he does not advocate, that a dualistic metaphysics is the true one? And, again, in the social field there are times to emphasize individualism and times to emphasize collectivism. In group relations there are times to urge compromise, and times to incite revolution. The principle of polarity has no magic key for solving these issues.

Cohen also gives ontological status to the principle of polarity when he insists that it is a "necessary copresence and mutual dependence of opposite determinations". Here the difficulty is even greater. There are areas and situations where polarity is exhibited. but there are many areas where the notion of polarity does not make any sense. The assertion that polarity is pervasive in the existential world must be settled by the empirical approach, and empirically there is no evidence for this assertion.

Finally, a few comments on Cohen's theory of ethics. By applying the principle of polarity to the field of ethics he reconciles absolutism and relativism. The absolutist is right in insisting that every choice "logically involves a principle of decision", and the relativist is right in insisting that "feeling or perception of the actual demands" of life must supply the content of our ethical decisions. Cohen's approach is both defensible and fruitful; it does justice to both the moral and critical demands.

His procedure would have been more persuasive if he had given us a more detailed account of the nature of moral standards or "oughts". Sometimes he suggests that reason will enable us to determine the moral standards and at other times he suggests that wisdom must do this for us. However fruitful these suggestions be, they are so general that they can hardly be said to deal with the age-old difficulties of ethical problems. Cohen insists on the uniqueness of the concept of the "ought", but how do we pass from the "is" to the "ought"? One would expect that Cohen as a naturalist would have established a much more vital connection between human desires and the "oughts". He favors hedonism to a limited degree, but to give a wider dimension to life he insists on the heroic virtues and the pursuit of unattainable ideals.

It is interesting to note that in advocating his list of desirable ends he does not make use of the principle of polarity. The virtues that stand high in his philosophy are contemplation, philosophic resignation, and the tragic sense, as against vital action, romantic venture, and the melioristic attitude.

These critical comments need not distract one from a deep appreciation of Cohen's vision of reality. Even if one may not wholly agree with his specific formulations, his devotion to truth, to scientific method, to a spacious metaphysics, to liberal causes, and his courage to face the darker aspects of existence should be a source of inspiration.

IV

SINGER'S PHILOSOPHY OF EXPERIMENTALISM

The central issue of philosophy is the theory of evidence. What basically differentiates philosophies is the differences in this theory. The philosophers who have a similar conception of evidence have, usually, similar world views, whereas those who differ in their conception of evidence have, usually, different world views. The major modern schools of philosophy—the rationalistic, the empirical, and the critical—are based on the theory of evidence that is peculiar to each of them. The late Edgar A. Singer, J.r, one of the most significant of recent American philosophers, deals with this theory in his major book *Experience and Reflection*, which has been published posthumously and edited competently by C. West Churchman, one of Singer's former students.

"Man's every act", Singer writers, "is an act of faith, generally, an unconscious faith; seldom, an examined faith : never, a faith that by taking thought could have been replaced by assured certainties".[1] And he rightly observes that nothing "can be more important to any man than to do all he can to assure the soundness of his reasons for the faith that is in him; i.e. to test the weight of evidence supporting the working hypotheses on which he is willing to act".[2] The core of Singer's contention is experimentalism. For an experimentalist there is no fact that is beyond the progressive procedure of experiment. As Singer expresses this principle in one of his earlier articles, "A question not answerable by experiment is meaningless".[3] The far-reaching consequences of this principle constitute his philosophy.

---

[1] *Experience and Reflection* (Philadelphia : University of Pennsylvania Press, 1959), p. 3.

[2] *Ibid.*, p. 3.

[3] "Philosophy of Experiment", *The Symposium*, Vol. I, 1930, p. 156.

Before presenting his experimental theory of evidence, Singer examines what rationalism, empiricism, and criticism have to say on evidence. His comments on the historic systems of evidence are penetratingly critical. His discussion of Kant is especially significant, and much more enlightening than most of the traditional accounts. He finds in the views of evidence from Leibnitz to Kant what strikes him as a dialectic, yet not in the Hegelian sense of an infallible means of discovery but rather in the psychological sense of a progressive debate.

The present discussion will consist of three parts : first, Singer's experimental theory of evidence will be examined; secondly, the application of experimentalism to life will be analyzed; and, finally, something will be said on the relation of experimentalism to mind, social group, and value. Unfortunately, in the present book Singer had not reached the discussion of these latter concepts, but he had treated them in earlier books.

I

Singer starts his analysis of experimentalism from the common saying, "we learn by experience". But experience is a weasel word since it may suggest inaccessible privacies and inarticulate immediacy. It is true that whatever one learns is based on experience, but one must possess certain prerequisites that make learning possible. Singer makes a distinction here : the experience belongs to one subject (the learner); the prerequisites that make learning possible to another (the reflective onlooker). The reflective onlooker may be another mind or one's own mind. Thus, *"every experiencing mind presupposes a reflective mind"*.[4]

The concept of reflective mind leads Singer to the analysis of the meanings of question and answer, or, more specifically, to the meanings involved in the empirical question of fact and the answers thereto. Singer begins by distinguishing between an answer and a response to a question. For example, to the question concerning the measurement of an angle, the answer is that the angle in question is one of $n°$; the response is that the angle measured is to be taken as one lying within the range $(m \pm p)°$. These two statements differ in all three of their grammatical parts : subject, predicate, and coupling verb. The

[4] *Ibid.*, p. 68.

subjects are, respectively, "the angle in question" and "the angle measured"; the predicates are "an angle of n°" and "an angle lying within the range $(m \pm p)°$"; the coupling verbs are "is" and "is to be taken as". Singer generalizes these differences between answer and response in relation to the basic concepts of science.

The first thing to be realized is that the scientist, when seeking answers to questions of fact, is governed by certain presuppositions. In his experimental work he is always limited to response, and a response, as has just been indicated is an assertion in the imperative mood, never in the indicative. There is the command, for instance, "Let the angle measured be taken as lying in the interval $(m \pm p)$". That science is the logic of imperatives has been argued by Kant, Poincaré, Duhem, and others. Singer agrees with this view and presents his own specific formulation of it. For Singer there can be no facts in any acceptable sense without presupposing logic, geometry, kinematics, and mechanics. Yet these presuppositions are not to be regarded as mere inductive generalizations, as Mill and other empiricists regarded them; they are to be interpreted in terms of their use and function in scientific inquiry. The matter of "gathering a responsive set is not entirely a matter of finding; it is, in ever increasing measure as science progresses, a matter of making as well".[5] The scientist finds that "he can *make* the ultimate data of his observation (e.g. instrument-readings) into something that, without his making, these data would not have furnished; namely, a response to a question of fact".[6]

Thus, the scientific pursuit is not a passive beholding and codifying of self-evident structures in things. On the contrary, the scientist moulds the plastic materials of observation to satisfy the ideals of science. "The exactest science is a poiesis, the experimenter with all his readings before him must turn 'maker', our last image of nature is a work of the scientist's art".[7] This making is never uniquely determined by any single set of empirical data; there are always alternatives from which choices are to be made. Nature is still the object of scientific knowledge, but only in the sense that a goal may be an object of endeavor. Nature for Singer is that image which science approaches as the error of observation approaches zero. Thus nature

---

[5] *Experience and Reflection*, p. 155.
[6] *Ibid.*, p. 156.
[7] *Mind as Behavior* (Columbus, Ohio, R.G. Adams & Co., 1924), p. 1x.

is not a Ding-an-sich, but the name of a certain ideal. "Nature is completed science. Science is nature in the making".[8]

In the light of the presuppositions involved in science, Singer's concept of the relation of law to fact can be rendered more definite by contrasting it with the notions of other schools. For the rationalist, knowledge of law does not imply knowledge of fact, but knowledge of fact implies knowledge of law. For the empiricist, all knowledge of law implies knowledge of fact, but some knowledge of fact does not imply knowledge of law. For the critical, some knowledge of law implies, and some does not imply, knowledge of fact; some knowledge of fact implies, and some does not imply, knowledge of law [9]. For Singer, every response to a question of fact implies the acceptance of a law and every response to a question of law implies the acceptance of fact. "Knowledge of law implies knowledge of fact. Knowledge of fact implies knowledge of law".[10] Newton's law of gravitation, for example, explains a host of phenomena; but the content of the law becomes meaningful when its equations are employed for interpreting matters of observation. And matters of observation become significant through the law.

The second thing to be considered in the scientist's quest for answers to questions of fact is the significance of the mechanical image. For Singer neither question nor answer exists now, yet each exists somewhere "in the limit". The schema he suggests to bring a question of fact nearer and nearer to the single-valued answer is the mechanical image. In the past, several kinds, of mechanics were proposed : the rigid connection pattern from Democritus to Newton ; the action-at-distance pattern from Newton on. These historic schemata differ in their geometry or in their kinematics or in both; yet Singer thinks that a common definition may be given to the mechanical schemata.

A mechanical schema, for Singer, is "a manifold of points (a) individuated by space-time coordinates, (b) classified in terms of certain structural properties, (c) and subject to mathematical conditions such that the values of all variables representing these coordinates and properties being given for any value of an independent variable, t, are determined for any second value of t".[11]

[8] *Ibid.*, p. 288.
[9] *Experience and Reflection*, p. 80.
[10] *Ibid.*, p. 83 and p. 195.
[11] *Ibid.*, p. 197.

A mechanical image of a natural system is a point image of that system, conforming to the requirements of a given mechanical schema[12]. Such an image provides many advantages. The series of observations to determine the value of a quantity at any one moment can be extended at will. The experimenter, by picturing his laboratory as a limited world, may "compose one intimate system so hung together in time and space, its points so mutually conditioned, as to allow him to construct in his workshop (both too big and too little) model after model of this world",[13] each model more accurate than the other. Though a given image will not always make possible the observations one anticipates, the experimenter is free to make new adjustments. If one assumed, for example, that the planets move in perfect circles, statistical inconsistencies would appear in a series of observations. In such situations, according to Singer, the experimenter must revise either (1) the image to which adjustment is to be made (a) as to pattern or (b) as to point distribution; or (2) the process of adjustment (a) as to method of adjusting or (b) as to data to be adjusted.[14]

There will, of course, be no one image that will provide a statistically consistent set of observations. The experimenter can choose some one image from what Singer likes to call a "permissible sheaf of images". The criteria suggested in this choice are varied, such as simplicity or convenience; but Singer suggests the pragmatic criterion of progressive revision. Finally, Singer's theory of the mechanical image does not have to commit itself to the notion of unique confirmation or disconfirmation. An image, to be acceptable, must yield statistically consistent observations. No one observation confirms or disconfirms a mechanical image; every given instance must be an integral part of a set of observations.

The third thing to be considered in the scientist's pursuit of answers to questions of fact is the relation between the real and the ideal. We should not be concerned merely with what scientists actually do, since they sometimes fail to be guided by the ideal of science, but rather with what they ought to do to get answers to questions of fact. The ideal of science, like all ideals, is a goal that one can never reach. As an illustration of an unattainable yet approachable goal, Singer refers to a series of rational values that never arrive at v2, yet

---

[12] *Ibid.*, p. 197.
[13] "Philosophy of Experiment", *The Symposium*, Vol. I, 1930, p. 161.
[14] *Experience and Reflection*, p. 212.

come nearer and nearer to the limiting conception. Singer, in the Kantian spirit, calls the limiting concept a *Grenzbegriff*, an *Idee* infinitely remote but approachable.

The experimentalist in his attempt to get answers to questions of fact seeks successive methods of which the aim is that "each successive method shall yield a response of the form R (m=p)v for which the value of v is higher than that of any response yielded by its predecessor".[15] This ideal of science, as De Sitter writes, "is always a struggle for the last decimal place, and the great triumphs of science are gained when, by new methods and new instruments, the last decimal place is made into the penultimate".[16]

Have we any assurance of the possibility of unlimited progressive approximation to the ideal of science? Here there are differences of opinion. Some maintain that in certain kinds of measurements we have already reached that decimal place which no new methods or new instruments can go beyond. Others maintain that nature is subject to an indeterminateness such that no experimental procedure can possibly come close to exactness; finally, others, and Singer is among these, unconvinced by the arguments behind both of these opinions, assert that science can make indefinite progress towards the ideal.[17]

The ideal of the scientist is a necessary postulate of his inquiry. This postulate is evidently no proposition to be accepted as true or rejected as false; it is a regulative principle, something to be accepted if agreeable to one's plans, or declined if disagreeable.

Singer defines fact, law, truth, reality in terms of the ideal of the experimentalist. The answer to a question of fact is single-valued. The answer, for example, to the question, What is the distance between A and B? is 1 unit, and 1 must be a uniquely defined number; yet obviously, such an answer to a question of fact is an ideal approachable but never attainable. The same thing is true of laws. The ideal is real in the sense that it explains the real world; and the real is ideal in the sense that it is the limiting concept in our pursuit of knowledge. Thus, Singer claims that idealism and realism are synthesized in scientific methodology. Singer's analysis of experimentalism is a significant contribution. His knowledge of science is authentic and substantial; his philosophic discussions are full of penetrating

---

[15] *Ibid.*, p. 181.
[16] Kosmos, Harvard University Press, 1932, p. 134. (Quoted by Singer.)
[17] *Experience and Reflection*, p. 176.

insights. His account of the presuppositions in science, which is central to his philosophy of science, is not hampered by Kantian rigidities nor mutilated by the classic empiricist's insistence that these presuppositions are inductive generalizations. The presuppositions of science are analyzed in the context of scientific activity and described in terms of their function in experimental inquiry.

Yet there are some issues in Singer's philosophy of science that demand greater clarification and more circumstantial treatment.

Singer makes out a persuasive case for the use of the mechanical image; it is one of his guiding principles. Yet it seems that he could have strengthened his contention if he had examined and justified it in relation to contemporary physics, especially quantum mechanics. Although the latter does not necessarily disrupt the determinism of the mechanical image that Singer proposes, yet there is an issue to be faced. Singer himself admits that this issue has split the scientists. It is true that Churchman in his introduction makes some interesting and relevant comments on this issue, but the great importance that Singer gives the mechanical image required a more detailed discussion under the circumstances.

And, again, the concept of the ideal which is central to Singer's philosophy of science is not altogether clear. Singer makes fruitful use of his conception of the ideal as an approachable though unattainable limit, but one is not sure whether one should regard it as a pragmatic, guiding principle or as an idealistic doctrine of reality. The ideal as a pragmatic, guiding principle is akin to Peirce's regulative principles, and as such is convincing and useful; but the ideal as an idealistic doctrine of reality demands a much more detailed defense, and at best is highly controversial. The ideal as an idealistic theory of reality seems to be a reformulation of Hegel's famous principle, "the real is rational, the rational is real", into "the real is ideal, the ideal is real". And he often wrote as an "empirical idealist". Yet one finds Singer's philosophy most defensible when one steers clear of the obscurities of the idealistic tradition and takes him as a naturalist with a pragmatic strain.

II

Singer carries his experimental procedure into the biological realm. Can living beings, their structure and their activities be explained in experimental terms? This has been a controversial issue for many centuries. On this issue Singer's theory is both original and significant. In many respects his discussion of the bearing of experimentalism on biology, though not completed in the present work, is his most important contribution.

His fundamental contention is that biological categories are both independent of and compatible with physical ones. For him, mechanism and teleology are compatible. He parts company with the two major schools in biology : with the mechanists, who would reduce all biological processes to models of mechanism; and with the vitalists, who would introduce non-physico-chemical entities, like Driesche's entelechy or Bergson's *élan vital*, and thus introduce a gap between mechanism and life.

Just how are mechanism and teleology compatible in biology? The first point to be noticed in this contention is that objects of experience may be classified in different ways for different experimental purposes. Singer suggests a relativistic theory of classification as against the absolutistic classification of the classic theory". ... the universe of classic logic has been replaced in modern logic by *this* universe and *that*; much as at some prehistoric time the horizon must have been replaced by your horizon and mine. To replace the one classic universe, we have come to recognize many a 'universe of discourse' ".[18] If relativistic classification is possible one may rightly entertain the view that some natural bodies may have properties belonging to contradictory classes. To possess contradictory properties is not the same thing as to possess properties belonging to contradictory classes. At a given moment in a "gravitational system, no body can have a mass of 1 gr. and a mass of 2 grs; or an acceleration of 1 cm. per s per s, and an acceleration of 2 cm. per s per s, but any body can have a mass of 1 gr. and an acceleration of 1 cm. per s per s. Yet in such a system, the mass of a body is, its acceleration is not, independent of environment; its mass is structural, its acceleration a non-structural property".[19]

With this principle in mind Singer discusses some of the significant types of classes—the mechanical, physical, morphological, and functional. These types of classes are designed by the experimentalists in their pursuit of knowledge; their value lies in serving their purpose. They are made by the experimentalists, yet they are not « arbitrary ».

[18] "Mechanism, Vitalism and Naturalism", *The Philosophy of Science*, Vol. 13, No. 2, (1946), p. 89.
[19] *Ibid.*, p. 90.

The second point to be considered is Singer's concept of producer-product; which is especially significant in connection with morphological classes. The relation of an acorn to the oak may be described in terms of cause and effect or of producer and product. In the cause-and-effect relation the prior conditions must be necessary and sufficient; in the producer-product relation the prior condition is necessary but not sufficient. The acorn and all the relevant environmental conditions are necessary and sufficient for the effect oak; but the acorn is a necessary but not sufficient condition for the production of the oak. The morphological class of acorns represents potential oak producers, some acorns are oak producing ones and some are not.

The third point to be considered in Singer's contention of the compatibility of mechanism and teleology in biology is his concept of function. For Singer functional classes group objects not on the basis of their structure—mechanical or morphological— but on the basis of common productive properties. More precisely stated, when there are "two or more morphologically different classes of potential producers, whose respective products fulfill an identical nonstructural condition, each of these classes is a species of the functional genus".[20] Thus acorns and eggs differ in their morphological structure, yet belong to the class of structures that have the common function of reproduction—acorns of oaks, eggs of birds : both are reproducers of the parents that produced them. Or, again, such structurally incompatible objects as the sundial, hourglas, the clepsydra, pendulum clock, the springwatch, and the electric oscillator are subsumed under the functional genus timepiece. The significant point is that such mechanically different objects when grouped in terms of their function exhibit new properties. Timepieces are susceptible of no structural or mechanical explanation; laws governing timepieces have no mechanical definition; under these laws, the past of a given timepiece may be explained, but its future cannot be predicted; the most probable function of any timepiece is a function of its past.[21]

But it should be emphasized that things or organisms can be classified both on the basis of structure and on the basis of function without running into the charge of incompatibility. Whichever basis is chosen depends upon one's immediate purpose.

---

[20] *Ibid.*, p. 95.
[21] *Experience and Reflection*, pp. 326-343.

Given the concept of function, what is its bearing on life? Although living beings are complete images of mechanism, they are nevertheless functional systems. How then shall we define life in functional terms? This is a difficult task. Singer examines some traditional definitions and finds them inadequate. Historically nutrition and reproduction are taken as normal if not universal manifestations of life. But it has been possible to show that some living things do not display one of the properties and that some non-living things display one of them. Seeing the failure of these attempts, Singer suggests the possibility of at least one functional property other than those of nutrition and reproduction which may be possessed only by living beings. But the function he suggests is assignable not to individuals but to a very general class.

To understand Singer's way of defining the functional nature of life, we may avail ourselves of an analogy that he uses. A juryman as an individual does not have the function of the class to which he belongs; he has that function only as a member of a group which collectively has a certain legal function. Similarly, the function of the living thing is the function peculiar to the class of which it is a member. Thus, for Singer, the definition of life is not to be framed in terms of a condition common and peculiar to all the norms to which the individual organism may conform; it is "to be framed in terms of the laws of heredity which are indeed common and peculiar to the organism and sequence of organisms composing an evolutionary line".[22]

In attempting to give a definition of life in terms of the laws of heredity Singer presents a detailed and complex discussion of the conditions for such a definition. These conditions are concerned with the patterns of development in bodies, links, chains, and lines. The discussion of these conditions is unnecessarily complicated and unfortunately not complete. Yet one gets the general direction of Singer's interpretation of life.[23]

The conditions that form the basis of Singer's definition of life will now be indicated. The growth of bodies must proceed through a series of states, such that the morphology specific to each state conforms to a common law. It should also be noted that the growth of bodies may be protogenic (having the common norm of the species),

[22] *Ibid.*, p. 373.
[23] *Ibid.*, p. 365.

or metagenic ((differing in form according to the Mendelian law). A sequence of bodies agreeing in their patterns of growth constitutes a link. A sequence of links joined together in such a way that they recapitulate one another constitutes a chain. A sequence of bodies in which each body is born of the one immediately preceding in the link constitutes a line. Singer adds other conditions in his final definition of life. A chain must have a sufficiently large number of factors for the potential production of certain morphologies and functions. The final result of all these conditions is that "all bodies composing a biogenic line and only such bodies will be *living* bodies or *organisms*"[24]. Singer's discussion of life in experimental terms is of special significance.

First of all, he tries to present a view that will do justice to the ideals of science as well as to the ideals of purposive activity. This dual aim will later be shown to bear directly on his notions of mind and value. for Singer, "the scientific demand that we treat nature as an inviolable mechanism and the ethical demand that the human element in nature remain free agent are consistent".[25] Mechanism and teleology refer to different ways of interpreting events. From the mechanical interpretation to the teleological there is a leap, but it is a leap from one attitude of the mind to another attitude, and not a violation of Nature's causal order. Both are legitimate, nor has either type of explanation priority or greater importance.

Secondly, the functional or teleological explanation is empirical. Singer's analysis of functional or purposive activities is not in terms of non-physical agencies or unobservable private drives, but in terms of experimental procedures and entities.

His approach to the notion of life being experimental, his concern is not primarily to formulate a definition that is common to all living beings but rather to find a model that is best suited to the purposes of the biologists. The meaning of a term may be determined either by giving the common invariant core of the term, or by formulating it within the postulate of the science to which the term belongs. Singer's approach to the meaning of life is of the second type. And just as the postulates of science are not unchangeable but are reconstructed because of new instruments or new tasks, so too the meanings of terms are not invariant.

[24] *Ibid.*, 365.
[25] *Modern Thinkers and Present Problems* (New York : Henry Holt & Co., 1923), p. 311.

III

Although experimentalism is a well established method in the physical sciences and is becoming more and more established in the interpretation of life, its application to mind, society, and human values is still controversial. In extending the experimental procedure to these areas, Singer has been one of the pioneers in this country. Had he completed the present book, he would no doubt have elaborated this aspect of the subject, but one can get from his other books his essential ideas on it.

According to him, mind is behavior. In his brilliant article "Mind as an Observable Object" (1910) he was the first American philosopher to maintain the behavioristic theory of mind, anticipating by two years John Watson's famous article "Behaviorism". In a series of subsequent articles he formulated one of the most adequate statements of this conception. At present the behavioristic approach to mind in its different forms is the dominant one in American psychology. Yet Singer's behaviorism is not a mechanistic theory of mind. For him the categories of life and mind are teleological. He argues that the category of mind must be given an objective account but this objectivity must be in terms of teleology. To do justice to the teleological aspect of mind one need not introduce vitalistic agencies; one need only reclassify the body on the basis of its behavior.

Singer's behavioristic theory of mind is primarily a relative one. To mind the attributes that superiority in resource which enables one life to win what another must lose. "If one living being can accomplish a given purpose in $(n+1)$ types of situation, another in but n of these, we call that (nonmechanical) quality in which the first is better equipped than the second a faculty of mind".[26] And to mind he also attributes that "wisdom or reasonableness in the choice of ideals which in all times has been taken to distinguish the philosopher from the man of no thought".[27] Finally, to mind he attributes the power of knowing another state of mind. Singer calls this phase of mind the conscious mind. In his own words, "Being conscious is the state of a mind knowing another state of mind".[28] Consciousness

---

[26] *Mind as Behavior*, p. 113.

[27] *Ibid.*, p. 164.

[28] "On the Conscious Mind", *The Journal of Philosophy*, Vol. XXVI, No 21, (1929), p. 574.

refers to the togetherness of knowledge. Mind as self-consciousness is knowledge, through memory, of one's own earlier experience; and mind as other—consciousness is knowledge of the experience of others. Yet conscious mind, as well as other aspects of mind, is a form of behavior and therefore observable.

Social groups are also to be described experimentally, that is, in terms of observable behavior. In this area Singer's discussion is sketchy, yet he presents the necessary principles of the empirical approach. The behavior of the social group is not to be identified with the behavior of any particular members, but is a new, emergent entity. Taking Singer's example, the average Parisian at the time of the Reign of Terror was an easy-going, witty, pleasant individual, but collectively he generated the spirit of the mob. And this new entity can be studied as scientifically as its constituents, in fact, we often get fruitful information about an individual by first examining the society to which he belongs.

Finally, human values are also to be approached experimentally. There has been a long tradition that would separate human values from nature and thus make them inaccessible to the scientific approach. Sometimes a supernatural belief was the barrier, and sometimes the fear that the scientific approach would annul the finer aspects of value. Singer's approach to human values is devoid of these obsessions. He is firmly convinced that to understand values one's analysis must be scientific in the large sense of the term. Generalizations about values can be arrived at by this method, so there is no need of any special kind of logic.

At this point one has to introduce a caveat. If science is to be a fruitful guide in the realm of values, it cannot be limited to description. The physical and behavioral sciences do not inevitably ensure the human race against the destructive possibilities of science, but they can provide the means for progress. At some point of the analysis of values, i.e. of moral values, one has to introduce a norm through which to determine the goodness or badness of actions. Singer is fully aware of this problem and introduces such a norm in his account of morality; and it is a norm within an empirical setting and therefore naturalistic in its implications .He finds that the deepest desire of human beings is to have the power to realize their potentialities. The imperative he suggests is : "So live the moment that every future moment may find you stronger than you would have been had you lived in any other way".[29] It is in the boundless possibilities of science and of social cooperation and of art that he finds the means to achieve this power. The major problem for the human race to solve is : "How construct a world, inhabited by many wills, in which each will pursuing its utmost desire shall in so doing serve to the utmost each other doing the same?"[28]

Singer's experimentalism is one of the most rigorous, coherent, and impressive of recent philosophic outlooks. Its relevance to the contemporary scene is such as to take it beyond limited philosophic circles. It is not a complete system, since no philosophy can be this. "We formulate in order to revise", he writes, "and when one of us is asked ... to account for his creed in terms of his life, what is left for him to do ... but to recall the dissatisfactions that have pushed him on, and are still pushing?" [30] Yet at a time when the arrogant claims of authoritarian dogmas suppress human progress, and when harsh anti-rationalistic attitudes hamper the rational approach to human problems, a philosophy like Singer's that combines the scientific procedure with humanism is very energizing.

---

[29] *In Search of A Way of Life*, (New York : Columbia University Press, 1948), p. 17.
[30] *On the Contented Life*, (New York : Henry Holt & Co., 1933), p. 184.

V

HOCKING AND THE DILEMMAS OF MODERNITY

Many are deeply aware that contemporary civilization is in travail. The root causes of this condition and the patterns of life that will finally emerge from the current political, ideological, and religious conflicts are highly ambiguous. Professor William E. Hocking, in his book *The Coming World Civilization*,[1] approaches these problems with a fully developed philosophic system and after a rich experience of world cultures. His analysis is many-dimensional, presenting significant comments on contemporary civilization and finely integrating the threads of the discussion.

Hocking's starting point is that our varied civilizations are moving, though unsteadily, towards a single world civilization. In this movement the state and the church—the religious community in all its forms—are the most important forces, since "each of these undertakes in its own way to reflect and satisfy the whole of human nature". Yet in pressing their roles these two institutions are involved in some basic incompatibilities. The state, despite its great power and public function, is unable to furnish by itself the necessary motivation for its vitality.

The state can apply penalties, but it cannot punish, since "only the man who has enough good in him to feel the justice of the penalty can be punished"; the state can build schools and organize and supervise instruction, but it cannot educate, since education depends on the personal qualities of teachers; the state can establish legal forms for the family, but it cannot mend by law the faltering spirit of creative love; the state can canalize and regulate the economic activity, but of "indolent human clay" it cannot "produce an industrious society";

---

[1] (New York : Harper and Brothers: 1956), xiv, 210 pp. The quotations are from this book unless otherwise indicated.

the state can control many aspects of recreation, but it cannot by itself prevent the degradation of leisure; the state can establish laws, but it "cannot from its own resources assure the soundness of its system of law".

Whence, then, shall come the motivation that is required for the maintenance of the vitality and integrity of the state? It is here that the function of the church comes in when broadly conceived. Religion, instead of tending to wither away, becomes increasingly necessary to the life of the state, for it is religion that provides our deeper motives and affirms the anchorage of our ideal ends in reality. Yet religion must function within the context of technical, scientific, and philosophic modernity. Unless modernity is to be regarded as retrogression, religion must be compatible with it, although not necessarily based upon the cornerstones of modernity.

This brings us to the central philosophic issue with which Hocking is concerned. Modernity, for him, presents certain major stumbling blocks or dilemmas in the path of religion trying to provide the necessary motivation. These dilemmas are the root troubles of contemporary civilization. What are these dilemmas?

The first one arises from subjectivity. Subjectivity, beginning most definitely with Descartes' "I think, therefore I am", gives us self-consciousness, our sense of individuality, yet develops into subjectivism, relativism, psychologism. And the second dilemma arises from the complement of subjectivity, namely objectivism. The latter, again beginning most definitely with Descartes' mechanical view of nature, gives us the abstract universals of science, yet develops into the night view of Fechner and the vision of the purposeless universe. Hocking's approach to the dilemmas is dialectic in the sense that he attempts to find the cure by carrying the logic of these dilemmas to the end; he thus wishes to do justice to their truth as well as to their error. His argument is an attempt to go beyond modernity without losing the modern depth of subjectivity and without depriving us of the abstractions of science; he would give universality to private experience, and a more integrated and unified knowledge than the sciences provide.

We shall examine how Hocking overcomes the dilemmas of subjectivity and objectivity, and proceed this idea of the Whole as the final synthesis of his dialectic. The discussion will be confined to his major philosophic claims. His illuminating comments on Christianity, on various world religions, and on the various aspects of civilization deserve a separate paper.

I

The first dilemma of modernity that Hocking exposes to dialectic analysis is subjectivity. This dilemma, to repeat, may be stated as follows : On the one hand, we cannot reject subjectivity since this has given us the modern idea of the individual and his rights; on the other hand, without universality in our private experience there can be no wholeness, no integrity of the individual. The issue therefore is : How can we keep the benefits that accrue from subjective depth and at the same time give to our experience universal validity?

Hocking's approach to this problem is within the idealistic tradition, although with certain modifications of his own. His argument for the universal validity of knowledge takes the form of dialectic. The starting point of our knowledge is taken to be sense-experience. In this experience we receive Nature, with all its qualities, ready-made and obstinate; this is the ground of natural realism. But natural realism is a limited and inadequate account of our knowledge. Knowledge of Nature implies immediate knowledge of other minds since what we face is a common, public, sharable world. Experience, modernity's favorite word, suggests an actual world-wide intersubjectivity, "such as would exist if the ego and its fellows shared an identical object". In sense-experience different minds literally coalesce in Nature. Yet this knowledge of other minds would not be possible if I had not immediate knowledge of yet another Mind which cannot be that of fellow human beings but is wholly creative in its knowing, i.e., Absolute Mind, God. Thus we know one another only because we first know God; this primal knowledge supplies the basis for the notion of social experience. This knowledge also makes possible the universality of judgment, for in intersubjectivity we find a ground for the "*nonsolitude of the solitary ego*". It should also be noted that God in creating Nature is also creating me; the empirical receptiveness to the sensed world is "a receiving of my own life from a life-giving entity. ... It is not a causing; it is a communicating; it is the primitive Thou-experience". In the incessant will of the empirical strand of living, always including sensation, the self is "being created".

Before considering some of the more debatable issues in Hocking's dialectic argument, it is worth noting that his notion of the intersubjectivity of a common world has certain advantages over the usual types of subjective idealism. Hocking's idealism is not committed to the unsharable privacy of Leibnizian monadology. When there is actual identity of sense-experience, there is a bridge for passing from self to another. As Hocking says, "*Solipsism is overcome, and only overcome when I can point out the actual experience* which gives me the basis of my conception of companionship". Yet it should be realized that subjectivism lurks deep in the companionship Hocking suggests. To this I will refer again.

It should also be pointed out that Hocking's emphasis on the social aspect of knowledge is valuable. Knowledge is social not only in the sense Dewey, Mead, and others argued, viz., that our concepts and thoughts are molded by language, bysocial and cultural interaction, but it is social also in the sense that its meanings must be communicable, its truth must be verifiable, its evidence must be demonstrable by one to another. Even the solitary mind in its pursuit of knowledge needs another mind—its own other. Knowledge always involves appeal to other minds, to other judgments. As Hocking aptly says, "Other Knower is an integral part of the simplest knowledge of Nature itself".[2] Yet this statement does not mean for Hocking mere communicability in the usual sense of this term.

We shall now turn to Hocking's more specific aspects of intersubjectivity. Intersubjectivity for Hocking involves sense-experience as a common ingredient of different minds, minds literally coalescing in Nature. Two minds similarly and simultaneously experience the same thing, that is, interpenetratingly. As Hocking says in one of his earlier books : "I am in thy *soul*. These things around me are in thy experience. They are thy own; when I touch them and move them I change *thee*. When I look on them I see what thou seest; when I listen, I hear what thou hearest. I am in the great Room of thy soul; and I experience thy very experience".[3] Each is in the soul of the other, or both are as in a "room". The same view is expressed in the present book : "In practice, each individual mind, having its unique perspective of a world, includes therein its fellow mind. ... Could there be such a thing as a veritable consubjectivity whereby one self participates, not by imaginative or symbolic construction, but by actual experience, in the selfhood of another? ... If that were the case, we should see and judge things with *a natural universality*". And it is "such a paradoxical immediacy of otherness" that solves for Hocking the dilemma of subjectivity.

---

[2] *The Meaning of God in Human Experience* (New York : Yale University Press, 1912), p. 269).
[3] *Ibid.*, pp. 265-266.

Such a fascinating view of intersubjectivity is only plausible if one starts with the presuppositions of subjective idealism. If objects as ideas, are part of my mind, then if I perceive an object which another mind perceives we each perceive a part of the mind of the other, and thus have immediate experience of other mind.[4] Here we have the original subjectivism, and it is also Hocking's. As he expresses it : "... physical experience, taken as a solitary experience, has no very perfect independence of my Self; is not so external but that it can at any moment be conceived internal to me".[5] This is, of course, a necessary step for Hocking toward his Absolute Idealism, yet it is that very subjectivism from which, once one is in its toils, no way has ever been found to quite enable one to escape.

If we look to the facts of our social experience, without the dubious presuppositions of subjective idealism, we do not have direct experience of our neighbor's experience. It is true that whatever experience my neighbor has is open to experimental investigation, and thereby available to me as knowledge. But to know the sensation or the experience of my neighbor I need not have his sensation or his experience : I need only determine the relations, the conditions and the consequences of his sensation or experience.

And, again, if one allows the possibility that in perception I am in active commerce with an independently existing object, as seems to be the case, though my mind always brings something to my experience—classifications, interpretations—there is no difficulty in concluding that two minds can experience the same thing simultaneously without interpenetration. Each observes the same thing for himself.

Secondly, the notion of intersubjectivity involves, for Hocking, the idea of a universal other Mind that is the sustainer of the universality of our judgments and that in creating Nature is also creating me. Here, again, Hocking's subjectivism is quite palpable. The universal other Mind is posited by him because he refuses to entertain the view that objects may exist independent of the knowledge of some subject or that the sense of reality is possible apart from "shared ideas". But if the more realistic approach to intersubjectivity is acceptable, then there is no necessity for a cosmic other Mind as the sustainer of the universality of our judgments or as the creator of

---

[4] D.C. Macintosh, *The Problem of Knowledge* (New Haven : Macmillan & Co., 1915), p. 171.
[5] *The Meaning of God in Human Experience*, p. 284.

Nature. Nature is the ground of our universality and there is no need
to go beyond Nature. Nothing is gained in intelligibility by resorting
to super-Nature. By introducing a universal other Mind to explain
the existence of Nature, Hocking is merely inviting the question.
What is the reason for the existence of the universal other Mind?
To avoid this question he resorts to the notion of mystery : "... to
know that we cannot know may be our most significant knowledge";
or, again, "The term mystery ... aids to conserve the sense of wonder
without which human experience ceases to be human, and which
philosophy, in understanding, should enhance, not dissipate".[6] One
need not discard this mood, but why not apply it to Nature? If we
are going to end in mystery, nothing is gained by going beyond
Nature.

Hocking also claims that our response to the sensed world is not
merely to a physical stimulus but to a life-giving entity. In this experience my self is being created. And "whatever creates a self can only
be a self". One may agree with him that the response to a stimulus
is not merely a mechanical action; since it involves anticipatory
elements, it is to this extent teleological; but to say that in my encoun-
ter with my sensed world my self is growing, developing, and
therefore, if you like, is being created is no reason for believing that
the source of my sensed world must be a self. The natural conditions
of my environment, of my organism, of my social milieu give me a
sufficiently intelligible account of my growth, of my "being created".

II

The second dilemma of modernity which Hocking considers is
the objectivity that is presupposed in the scientific method. We need
the abstract universals of science, yet if these are the "Real" our
human purposes find no objective support. Hocking's dialectic analysis attempts to show the limitations of science and the necessity
of going beyond science to find a ground for the meanings of life.

First, as to the nature of scientific abstractions. From Hocking's
point of view science deprives nature "not alone of all purpose in the
shape of 'final causes', but as well of all quality and value". From the

---

[6] "Marcel and the Ground Issues of Metaphysics", *Philosophy and Phenomenological Research*, Vol. 14 (1953-1954), p. 449, footnote.

scientific standpoint the cosmos we live in is purposeless and devoid of qualities; it is a realm of fact and event ideally mathematical in structure and process, ideally devoid of meaning. The image of Nature that we get from science is what Fechner called the "night view" of nature—"that purposeless and qualityless cause-tight universe which a perfected science, including the sciences of man, would insist upon". Such a universe, for Hocking, is the negation of all religion in the sense of a cosmic call to right living, or as the rootage of man's values in reality.

Hocking, of course, does not discard a limited use of science. Scientific abstraction, or the "night view" of nature, is for him an achievement of first magnitude. This conception has been made possible by the mathematical genius of modernity and by a host of empirical observers. Scientific abstraction is necessary not only for the community of scientists, but for all of us. Human beings are free to utilize for their innumerable purposes only what is non-purposive; they can exploit for their ends without consideration and compunction only what is inanimate. Hocking, therefore, disagrees with panpsychists like Fechner and Whitehead, who seek to remedy the vacuousness of physical nature's structure by ascribing to it universal animation.

Yet scientific abstractions, for Hocking, are intrinsically limited. Science in its zeal has made or has implied metaphysical assertions to which it has no right: that nature as mathematically conceived is the whole of reality; that what empirical science can show is the only acceptable truth; that what the science of man can show of man is the whole of man. From Hocking's point of view a scrupulous empiricism would refrain from such assertions. A more truthful science would admit that in the strict sense of the term there is no scientific account of reality, that science gives only abstractions, and that there is no science of man, but only science of the robot.

Hocking is right in pointing out the abstract nature of scientific description. He is also right in rejecting the view that scientific abstractions are the only genuine realities and that experienced qualities are mere appearances. But what he asserts about the implications of scientific abstraction in relation to one's philosophy is highly questionable.

First, it is worth pointing out that abstraction by itself need not be rejected; it neither distorts facts nor limits our knowledge. All responsible cognitive activities make selections and distinctions in their attempt to understand a situation; certain aspects of a situation are considered to be relevant and others not. In this sense all cognition involves abstraction, unless cognition is to be identified with intuition or the reduplication of experience.

And, again, though scientific knowledge is abstract, the abstractions do not involve the denial of qualities or values in our common world. Science begins within the matrix of our common world and comes back to it. What science is concerned with is not the denial of the qualities and values of events but the determination of the conditions under which events are generated.[7] The existence of water and its properties depends on certain chemical elements interrelated in definite ways; yet in determining these conditions one does not deny the distinctive properties of water. Similarly the occurrence of a color, say blue, depends on certain physical conditions, on electromagnetic vibrations of a certain wave-length; yet in determining these conditions one does not reduce the color blue to electro-magnetic vibrations.

Hocking's rejection of scientific abstractions finds its fullest expression when science attempts to understand man. He maintains that "there is no science of man; there is science only of the manikin, the robot". Science must stop at the portals of living beings, and especially of man. Man embodies a duality, "the events which are his life flow both from reasons (including ends) and from causes; but they flow from causes only by the consent of his reasons. ... The life process of man is end-seeking". If one means by science a certain specialized technique that is only used in physics and chemistry one may agree with Hocking's objection to science. But if by science we mean, as we usually do, certain general methods of getting evidence and evaluating it, then there certainly is a science of man. All aspects of man—his feelings, his thoughts, his purposive activities—are open to the experimental, verifying procedure that is characteristic of science.

Empirically, mind is a manifestation of the processes of nature. Mind occurs at a certain level of complexity in physico-chemical organic structure. This assumption neither denies nor belittles the specific properties of the mind or of human beings. What it requires is, first, a careful analysis of the physico-chemical, organic processes at the basis of the mind, and, second, a careful description of the specific

---

[7] E. Nagel, "Malicious Philosophies of Science", in *Sovereign Reason*, (Glencoe, Ill., The Free Press, 1954), pp. 17-35.

traits which mental beings exhibit, such as sensation, feeling, thinking, and willing. All these traits can be described experimentally and naturalistically.

Hocking is especially concerned with the contrast between the causal and the purposive aspects of man. Man has "a duality", and the life process of man as "end-seeking" goes beyond science. Against the mechanists we would agree with Hocking that in describing the nature of man we should not deny his end-seeking activities, but we would equally insist that these activities are natural processes. For certain purposes human actions may be described in causal terms; for other purposes the observable behavior of man may be so classified that, ignoring the causal conditions, actions may be described in relation to ends or goals. These two types of explanation are consistent, equally useful, and equally experimental.

III

Hocking provides a way of escape from the abstractions of science —through the unity of the Whole. One must attain a "personal intimacy of the whole" to get the full meaning of life and to establish anchorage in reality.

The Whole, for Hocking, is the ultimate and independent being on which other beings depend. The Whole is in a sense other than Nature, myself, and my fellow beings; yet it includes all these insofar as they are its created work.

The Whole, as the Absolute Self, also gives meaning and value to existence. Meaning and value are mere abstractions if independent of some mind; they can only be intelligible in relation to the Absolute Self. The mere factual aspect of things, evil itself, acquires rationality only when viewed and organized in the context of the Whole. Because man as metaphysician is "concerned with the real, he is bound to be concerned with the Whole".[8] Neither the human mind nor the human will can be content with part of reality; to aspire to union with the Whole is a characteristically human trait.

But how do we come to know the Whole? The knowledge of the Whole, according to Hocking, eludes the usual scientific cognition,

---

[8] Hocking, "Metaphysics : Its Function, Consequences, and Criteria", *The Journal of Philosophy*, Vol. XLIII, July 4, 1946, p. 372.

which is, for him, merely descriptive. Knowledge of the Whole can only be grasped in feeling, though this feeling is not devoid of ideas. Hocking calls this approach to reality "the ontological empiricism of feeling". " 'Experience', once considered as a process of sense awareness, is now recognized as a process of awareness of the real, not in spite of its inescapable feeling-component but *because of it*. Experience is passion-laden, and the passion in it is not without pertinence to the nature of the world it reports". In the higher reaches of cognition of the Whole, one attains understanding through mystical experience. This is the higher form of empiricism. "The personal answer—the mystic's answer—is the genuine empiricism, to those who find it, sufficient and unlosable, and at the same time in its nature valid for all".

The first thing to be noticed is that reality is incurably pluralistic and contingent. We never face the Whole that Hocking is concerned with. There are relative systems of wholes like the molecule, the organism, the family, the state, but the Whole as one integrated, meaningful totality is not within our experience. At best such an idea of totality may be considered as a regulative ideal in our pursuit of knowledge. Nature is in a sense such a regulative whole for the scientist. Nature may be taken as the ideal of completed science. But here the whole idea is the ideal limit which one may approach but never reach.

Yet Hocking suggests a method of knowing the Whole—through feeling. This suggestion has some value, though it should not be offered as a new way of knowing. It is true that sometimes one's feeling may be one's best guide, yet this efficacy of feeling has its own empirical grounds. In some cases where a certain action has led us to a successful result, a tendency is established between such actions and their expected results. So when a similar situation occurs there is a pleasant feeling tone, assuring us of the safety of the action we are about to perform. In such situations, feeling is at best a source of suggestion for a working hypothesis; the final court of appeal must still be the verified consequences of the action.

As for Hocking's higher form of knowledge of the Whole through mystical experience, this, too is an empirical issue. It is true that some have claimed to have had the mystical experience, a sense of oneness with the Absolute, but the alleged truth-value of mystics cannot be taken for granted on the basis of their own testimony. The truth claimed must be critically examined in the light of larger contexts, in relation to verifiable, external evidence. And the available verifiable evidence tends to deny the claim of the mystic. Hocking is not unaware of this situation : "... the mystic in reporting what he has experienced, has attributed to the objects of his experience some qualities which belong rather to his inner state. ... Is it not more than probable that those words, 'one, immediate, ineffable', which describe the Reality of the 'negative metaphysics', are in their first intentions descriptions of the mystic's inner experience? ... There is a wide difference between saying, 'My experience of Reality is ineffable' (passing my present powers of expression) and saying, 'Reality is ineffable' (without predicates)".[9] This criticism is crucial. And for Hocking mysticism need not escape theoretical problems; he subjects it to logical and psychological analysis. He adds rational thoughts to mysticism.

One need not ignore the rich values involved in mysticism. And no one in contemporary thought has made us more aware of these values than Hocking. He has eloquently expounded the fruits of mysticism—the desire to attain some supreme good, the spirit of attachment and detachment, the renewal or human energies. But need these values be based on highly debatable metaphysical assumptions? It is true that in the past those who have followed the truths of science and those who have followed the intuitions of mystics have lived religiously apart. Yet need it be so? "What ... if mysticism", writes a recent philosopher, "were to come to see that no heart's desire could be so certain of its object, but that the hope of winning this object must depend on the measure of its science? And what, again, if science were to bring itself to admit that no end of ambition could be so demonstrably worthy, but that the courage to pursue this end must be in need of incessant renewal?"[10] Certainly many have found in art the mystic's rapture and source of renewal, yet they have refused to surrender the intelligent direction of life to the intuitions of the mystics.

Hocking's major purpose in resolving the dilemmas of modernity is to clear the way for religious experience, which is regarded by him as the source of our ideal motives. One must agree with him that the integrity of civilization needs some source of motivation. On this

<hr/>

[9] The Meaning of God in Human Experience, pp. 352-354.
[10] Edgar A. Singer, Jr., On the Contented Life (New York : Henry Holt & Co., (1936), pp. 234-235.

issue he has significant suggestions. It is his hope that the growing unity of the unlosable essences, meaningful varieties, and converging purposes of the historic religions may bring a new vitality into the disturbed motivation of mankind. The values Hocking emphasizes are of major importance to our civilization. And it is quite possible for many who cannot accept the intellectual commitments of the historic religions to integrate most of the values that Hocking offers into the fabric of a humanistic religion.

VI

BRAND BLANSHARD'S RATIONALISTIC IDEALISM

In the present era the anti-rationalistic forces have been dominant factors. Reason has often been impotent in dealing with the passions of individuals, in reconciling the conflicts of economic and political groups, and in harmonizing the interests of races and nations. Yet many desire the healing guidance of reason. Among contemporary philosophers Brand Blanshard has been one of the strongest advocates of reason. In his writings as well as in his activities he has championed reason against the destructive forces of irrationalism. In this pursuit we would be happy to join him. But Blanshard as a philosopher has developed a rationalistic idealism which goes far beyond the usual use and meaning of reason, an aspect which deserves an independent examination.

I

Idealism has had a long and distinguished history. Any attempt to give an adequate definition of idealism which would cover all of its types and variations would be unfeasible. Yet in a most general way one may describe idealism as an attempt to interpret reality in terms of human aspirations and all the higher human categories. As mind and spirit are among the higher categories, idealists have interpreted reality in terms of varied meanings of mind and spirit. For some idealists reality is a group of sensations, for others it is universal will, and for still others it is reason or a rational system. Idealists have also differed in their emphasis on the plurality or the oneness of reality. For Blanshard reason is the key concept, and the structure of reality for him is an integrated, unified rational system. His philosophy may therefore be rightly called rationalistic idealism.

For Blanshard, not unlike Hegel and neo-Hegelians like Bradley and especially Bosanquet, the real is rational. Yet this simple claim has layers of meaning.

The real is rational in the sense that everything is internally related and interdependent. Everything is connected necessarily with everything else. All relations are internal, they form a network of unbroken implications. Not only terms but all events are also internally related by the causal relation, and this relation, for Blanshard, amounts to being a logical relation.

The universe for Blanshard is not a mere heap of things thrown together in hit-or-miss fashion, but a network of logical relations ultimately forming a single system or Whole. The system is self-sufficient and self-dependent, needing no agency over and above itself. In this respect Blanshard's monistic idealism differs from theism as well as from pluralistic idealism. His system also differs from psychological idealism in the sense that reality for him is inherently a logical system, not in the Platonic sense but in the sense that reality forms a logical stability. As Bosanquet points out, with which Blanshard would agree, " 'The driving force of Idealism', as I understand it, is not furnished by the question how mind and reality can meet in knowledge but by the theory of logical stability, which makes it plain that nothing can fulfill the conditions of self-existence except by possessing the unity which belongs only to mind".[1] Here there is a significant difference between Bradley's Absolute as a universal experience and Bosanquet's and Blanshard's Absolute as a realistic logical system.

The goal of reason for Blanshard is understanding, and under-. standing is grasping the necessary connections that constitute a system. The relation between idea and object must be conceived teleologically "as the relation of that which is partially realized to the same thing more fully realized. When we say that an idea is *of* an object, we are saying that the idea is a purpose which the object alone would fulfil".[2]

Truth in such a philosophy is coherence, and by coherence Blanshard means more than consistency. Coherence for him would mean the necessitation by each part and all the parts of the system. A given judgment is true "in the *degree* to which its content could maintain itself in the light of a completed system of knowledge, false in the

[1] *Logic*, 2d ed., (Oxford, Clarendon Press, 1911), p. 322.
[2] *The Nature of Thought* (London; George Allen & Unwin. Ltd., 1964), Vol. I, p. 473.

degree to which its appearance there would require its transformation"[3]. In a coherent system the integration would be so complete "that no part could be seen for what it was without seeing its relation to the whole, and the whole itself could be understood only through the contribution of every part".[4]

As for aesthetic and ethical values, here too the notions of necessity and the whole are important. Necessity is a relation between the parts of a whole imposed by the nature of the whole. There are all sorts and dimensions of the whole. Different types of values have each their system or whole which determines their standards. An artist's work, for example, is sound to the degree that he manages "to keep what is merely subjective and personal in abeyance, in short, because his brush has been under dictation from his subject".[5] And in morality necessity in the form of causality governs human action, but as there are levels of causality there is no reason whatever to suppose that moral choices are mechanically determined. Moreover, Blanshard does not pass as many idealists do from " 'everything is rational', in the sense of necessity, to 'everything is rational', in the sense of right".[6] For him necessity applies to everything, whereas goodness applies only to the experience of sentient beings.

II

Blanshard offers several arguments in favor of his rationalistic idealism. Three important ones will be examined : 1. A priori evidence or the demand for intelligibility; 2. Empirical evidence or the doctrine of internal relations; 3. Causality or the logical entailment of causal connections. The final result of these arguments culminates in the logically structured system of the Whole.

1. A priori evidence or the demand for the intelligibility of reality. The belief that reality is intelligible has undoubtedly been one of the major ideals in the development of science and philosophy. Whitehead has emphasized this ideal with special clarity : "There can be no living science", he writes, "unless there is a widespread instinctive conviction

---

[3] *Ibid.*, Vol. II, p. 304.
[4] *Ibid.*, p. 266.
[5] *Ibid.*, p. 436.
[6] *Reason and Analysis* (La Salle, Ill. : Open Court Publishing Co., 1962), p. 491.

in the existence of an *Order of Things*, and, in particular, of an *Order of Nature*".[7] Blanshard similarly advocates this ideal. For him reason demands complete intelligibility prior to experience. "Throughout the career of thought, from its first tentative appearance in perception to the flights of speculative reason, there is a single continuous drive toward intelligible system, a system which as all-comprehensive, is logically stable, and as perfectly integrated, leaves no loose ends".[8]

There are, of course, different types of intelligibility—the mechanistic, the teleological, and the theistic. For Blanshard intelligibility means a completely logical or necessitarian system. "The world could be accounted intelligible only if it were a system, all-inclusive and perfectly integrated, and that such integration would be achieved only if the parts were internally related".[9]

There are two general notions involved in Blanshard's belief that reality is intelligible, reality has a completely logical order or structure and that this order or structure is knowable.

As for the first notion, is Blanshard's belief that there is an all-inclusive and perfectly integrated logical system a necessary belief? That there is a certain degree of intelligibility seems a necessary belief, but that the whole of reality is without any element of contingency and is a totally logical interrelated system is an over-belief. Reason itself may indicate certain limits of reason. Beyond the demand for logical unity there is the more fundamental demand to take things as they are whether they satisfy one's preference for unity or not. And there are contingent elements in existence which do not favour Blanshard's extreme rationalism.

First of all, in every explanation there are relevant facts and irrelevant facts. The acceleration of gravitation depends on mass and distance and everything else is indifferent to it; the freezing of water depends on temperature and pressure and nothing else is relevant. Morris Cohen, after mentioning these facts, and many similar ones could be indicated, concludes, "To hold seriously to the popular dictum that everything is connected with everything else would make the scientific search for determinate connection meaningless".[10] Blanshard is not unaware of this difficulty; but he tries to overcome

---

[7] *Science and the Modern World* (New York, The Macmillan Co., 1948), p. 5.
[8] *The Nature of Thought*, Vol. II, p. 428.
[9] *Ibid.*, Vol. II, p. 475.
[10] *Reason and Nature* (New York, Harcourt, Brace and Company, 1931), p. 151.

it by insisting that everything, if not directly, is indirectly related to everything else. But this is a tour de force assertion of one's belief rather than meeting the specific objection.

Secondly, in every explanation there are data and facts which are contingent and these data and facts are to be discovered by observation and experimentation and not by mere reasoning. Sometimes reason may deduce certain data, but this depends on the given prior data. A group of material particles may gravitate to form one body, and one may subject this to rational explanation by law, yet laws operate on a given distribution of particles. Logical implication which proceeds from premise to conclusion must stem from a premise. We may go as far as we may by logical implication, but ultimately Blanshard's rationalism cannot generate being.

Thirdly, laws of nature are contingent. Why the particular laws of nature are and not others cannot be answered without assuming a certain contingency in nature. These are undemonstrated premises. Even if one could derive the laws of nature from one basic law, that law would be contingent. Ultimately the universe has the specific character it has and not some other; this contingent element cannot be removed through reason.[11]

The second notion involved in the intelligibility of reality as a logical system is that this system is knowable. This issue is a complex and difficult one. C.D. Broad, in discussing this issue in relation to the attempt of natural scientists to discover the order of nature, states three necessary postulates. First, the proposition that the world is intelligible involves the proposition that the world must obey the laws of logic; secondly, the naturalists must be able to disentangle them; finally, our sensations must come in an order that reveals the laws of nature.[12] Other aspects of this issue have been discussed by Norman Campbell and Poincaré. Blanshard short-cuts these complex issues by passing from the "immanent end" of thought to thought's "satisfaction". The "immanent end" of thought for him is a system at once rationally perfect and all-embracing, and the satisfaction of thought is the reality of his system. He thinks the «immanent end» of thought must be fulfilled in its "actualization". This argument is akin to the ontological argument for God in the sense that the idea of perfection has to exist *in re* as well as *in intellectu*.

---

[11] *Ibid.*, p. 152.

[12] *The Mind and Its Place in Nature* (London, Routledge & Kegan Paul Ltd., 1951), pp. 507-508.

For Blanshard, as earlier discussed, the relation between idea and object must be conceived teleologically, "as the relation of that which is partially realized to the same thing more fully realized" ; idea is a purpose which the object alone would fulfil. One may tentatively accept this description of the relation of idea to its object. But from this claim it does not follow that the object is what Blanshard asserts it to be. C. Watts Cunningham rightly describes this problem. He says, „ ... the structure of the object is logically prior to the "actualization" of the idea. But this is no warrant that the object must be an all-inclusive system".[13] He further asks the question, "Is it not a flat self-contradiction to determine important ontological features of 'the immanent end of thought' merely by appealing to thought's satisfaction before the eventuality of its 'actualization'?"[14] The idea must discover what it is and not impose its demands on it. This is the distinction between responsible thinking and wishful thinking.

What, then, is the result of Blanshard's attempt to establish our knowledge of the intelligibility of reality as a perfect logical system from the "immanent end" of thought to its "actualization?" It is obvious that he has not established this claim. This claim is based on faith, as he finally admits. It is a paradoxical situation that rationalists who are usually critical of assertions of faith should end up with faith as an aspect of their philosophy. Blanshard, of course, might say that his faith is a rational faith, but here, again, one detects his commitment to reason as ultimate value, which others may not accept.

It is true that our basic values and demands function as a priori principles in guiding our experience. These values or demands are posited a priori as *justificanda* rather than as *justificata*. We try to mould reality by these principles. Yet they are not ultimate or unalterable. They cannot be held in the long run unless they receive certification by the facts.

2. Empirical evidence or the doctrine of internal relations. The second argument which Blanshard offers for his rationalistic idealism is the empirical one, in many respects the most important one. The empirical argument is based on the doctrine of internal relations. And a relation is said to be "internal to a term when in its absence the

---

[13] *Philosophical Interrogations* : Sydney and Beatrice Rome. Edited (New York, Chicago, San Francisco, Holt, Richard & Winston, 1964), p. 247.

[14] *Ibid.*, pp. 247-248.

term would be different".[15] For Blanshard everything is internally related to everything else and the totality of connections forms a coherent system. Stated in greater detail, Blanshard means by internal relation "(1) that every term, i.e. every possible object of thought, is what it is in virtue of relations to what is other than itself;(2) that its nature is affected thus not by some of its relations only, but in differing degrees by all of them, no matter how external they may seem; (3) that in consequence of (2) and of the further obvious fact that everything is related in *some* way to everything else, no knowledge will reveal completely the nature of any term until it has exhausted that term's relation to everything else".[16] This is certainly a far-reaching claim !

The concept of relation is an ambiguous one. It has varied meanings. As John Dewey points out, "(1) Symbols are 'related' directly to one another; (2) they are 'related' to existence by the mediating intervention of existential operations; (3) existences are 'related' to one another in the evidential sign-signified function".[17] These three meanings of relation are different and unless they are clearly distinguished the use of the same word tends to create confusion. Blanshard in his discussion of internal relation does not make these distinctions very clear; yet what seems to be central to his doctrine is that reason demands that reality be a system of mutual implications, or, technically put, that all relations are internal to their terms. That there are internal relations between many terms may be admitted, such as father and son, husband and wife, north and south, 6 and 12, and many similar relations in geometry and mathematics; but the claim that in all empirical situations such relations must exist is not convincing.

I have before me on my desk Blanshard's *The Nature of Thought*, the two volumes covered with deep red wrappers. I change their positions and I further cover one of them with a blue wrapper. A number of spatial and atomic changes have happened between the two volumes; yet these changes have absolutely no relevance to the content of the volumes. And yet if certain chapters were destroyed in the first volume, they would have a significant bearing on the chapters of the second volume, since the destruction would disrupt the continuity of meanings.[18]

---

[15] *The Nature of Thought*, Vol. II, p. 451.

[16] *Ibid.*, p. 452.

[17] *Logic, Theory of Inquiry* (New York, Henry Holt and Company, 1938), p. 55.

[18] For a similar illustration, Charles A. Baylis, "Internality and Interdependence", *The Journal of Philosophy*, XXVI (1929), p. 374.

In a given context only some of the characters of an object are essential and others are accidental. We may put the issue pragmatically. Pragmatically, as William James argues, "... *the only meaning of essence is teleological.* ... The essence of a thing is that one of its properties which is so *important for my interests* that in comparison with it I may neglect the rest".[19] Or to put the same idea in different words, the classification of the properties of an object depends on our purpose. A dagger in one context is a weapon, in another an object of beauty; a book may be big in size, yet small in its meaningful content; a living being in one context is a physico-chemical system, in another a goal-seeking creature. Objects have different properties and their essence depends on how they are regarded in reference to our purpose.

Terms in new relations may get secondary properties without modifying or changing their determined primary property. A patch of red color may be used as a sign to stop cars or it may function as the symbol of a flag. The moon as a planetary object may become a target for the astronauts to land on, or the moon as light may be conducive to the romantic mood. Yet these secondary properties do not modify or change the determined primary property of the red as color, or of the moon as a planetary object.

Blanshard makes much of the relation of difference in relation to internal relations. According to him, "everything is related to everything else by the relation of difference at least. If it were not so related, it would clearly not be the thing it is, since then it would not differ from that which is admittedly other than itself. But a relation that could not be theoretically changed without changing the thing itself is precisely what we mean by an internal relation. Whence it follows that everything is related internally to everything else".[20]

This argument with its simplicity is impressive but on further analysis untenable. The major difficulty with this argument lies in the fact that unless the terms are internally related as in husband and wife, or in north and south, the absence or destruction of the relation of difference is merely an additive property to the primary meaning.

Being is the opposite of non-being and permanence is the opposite of change, and circle differs from triangle and color from tone. Yet

---

[19] *The Principles of Psychology* (New York, Henry Holt and Co., 1918), Vol. II, p. 335.
[20] *The Nature of Thought*, Vol. II, pp. 476-477.

the relations of opposition and difference are in no sense internal. Being implies non-being as a possibility just as non-being implies being, but the primary notions of being and non-being are not changed or modified by their opposition. It is not meaningless to conceive being without its opposite non-being, nor non-being without being. There is no necessary internal relation or transition in either notion. The same is true with respect to permanence and change. Neither of these are internally related except as possibility. One can imagine an unchanging quality, such as color without any alteration; and one can conceive change—a world obliterated—without any underlying permanence.[21] The oppositions both in being and non-being and in permanence and change are properties added to the primary properties.

Similarly, though circle differs from triangle and color from tone these relations of difference do not constitute internal relations. Circle has the same primary meaning with or without its relation to triangle; color has the same primary meaning with or without its relation to tone; their primary meanings would get an additive secondary meaning only where there are also triangles and tones.

The notion of difference is an important aspect of concrete individuals. Individuality emphasizes uniqueness, plurality, and a certain degree of externality rather than an all-inclusive internality or monism. In Blanshard's philosophy ultimately there is only one individual, the logical system, the Whole.

3. The third argument for the rationality of reality is based on the notion of causality as a logical entailment relation. For Blanshard there are two propositions about causality which would establish that everything in the universe is related to everything else. These two propositions are : " (i) that all things are *causally* related, directly or indirectly; (ii) that being causally related involves being *logically* related".[22]

Leaving the issue whether everything is causally determined—he dismisses the doubts that have been raised in recent physical theories about strict causality—I shall consider his claim that being causally related amounts to being logically related. He offers two arguments, a positive and a negative one.

The first, or the positive argument, is based on the claim that when-

---

[21] W.H. Sheldon, *God and Polarity* (New Haven, Yale University Press, 1954), p. 325.

[22] *The Nature of Thought*, Vol. II, p. 492.

ever we engage in inductive inference "the fact that the ground entails the consequent is one of the conditions determining the appearance of this consequent rather than something else in the thinker's mind".[23] In causal reasoning the thought of the premise, the cause (or part of the cause), logically necessitates the thought of the conclusion. There is thus an element of necessity in the causal relation.

There are difficulties in this theory. Ernest Nagel in discussing this issue points out several of them : a man who thinks that from a given premise he has drawn the logical consequence may in fact not have drawn the valid consequence; thoughts causally related do not necessarily stand in the relation of logical implication; sometimes a person without reasoning may luckily hit upon the conclusion; in this argument the relation between the notion of "necessary inference" and the necessary relation involved between propositions are confused.[24]

Blanshard admits most of these difficulties but insists that they do not invalidate his argument. The relation of ground to consequent, he asserts, is never a sufficient condition of inference. "The actual process of thought", he maintains, "is influenced by innumerable factors, by emotions, causal associations, suppressed and explicit desires, the state of the brain, general freshness or fatigue".[25] Yet he holds that when reason functions correctly "the logical relation between ground and consequent does serve, and can be directly seen to serve, as one of the conditions leading to the result".[26]

Limiting the issue to the occasions when reason functions correctly, the problem still remains whether in the cause and effect relation the premise logically necessitates the conclusion. Can we really speak of logical necessity in describing natural events? Logical necessity holds between propositions, between premise and conclusion, but not between the antecedent and consequent of natural events. The deductive method which flourishes in detecting necessities does not apply to the existential world. The method that is applicable to nature is observation, experimentation, verification. It is true that sometimes from a given hypothesis one may deduce unknown facts, but finally these facts must be checked and verified.

---

[23] *Ibid.*, p. 495.
[24] *Sovereign Reason* (Glencoe, Ill., The Free Press, 1954), pp. 287-89.
[25] *Philosophical Interrogations*, Edited by Sydney and Beatrice Rome, p. 232
[26] *Ibid.*, pp. 232-233.

Though the term logical necessity is not applicable to the cause and effect relation, there is coercion, compulsion, power in natural events. The hurricane that destroys trees and buildings, the fire that burns forests, the germs that destroy the body carry forceful results by their contingent properties. If one wishes to use the term necessity in connection with such happenings one may use the term physical necessity, which brings about results but does not carry the meaning of logical implication.

The second, or the negative, argument to which Blanshard gives considerable attention with some telling points is that one must accept either the regularity or the entailment view of causality. And as he thinks the regularity view is open to serious objections one should accept the entailment view. This argument is not convincing. Even if one should agree with most of Blanshard's criticism of the regularity view, this does not establish his case. There are a number of rival theories of causality which agree neither with the regularity view nor with the entailment view. To establish his claim for the entailment view Blanshard has to consider and refute not only one but all the other alternative views.

And it is worth noting that pragmatically the entailment view has no special advantage over the regularity view. In trying to determine the specific causes of events both theories have to examine past occurrences and present observable connections. The entailment view does not offer any new procedure to decipher the nature of events, or any new method to determine and predict specific causal happenings.

III

Blanshard's philosophy finds its final fruition in the idea of the Whole, which is a perfect, integrated, and logical system. This is the ultimate. The Whole is self-sufficient, self-dependent, with no agency to support it. That reality is in one sense a whole may be admitted, but the issue is, in what sense is it a whole? Nature or reality may be a whole in Blanshard's sense as an integrated, logical unity; or it may be a whole and diffused, "distributed, in the form of an indefinitely numerous lot of *eaches*, coherent in all sorts of ways and degrees".[27] Blanshard's arguments—a priori, empirical, and causal—were not able to prove the reality of a perfectly rational

[27] William James, *Pragmatism* (New York, Longman, Green & Co., 1913), p.264.

system. We do not even have in sub-systems like the family, the state, or the nation a fully integrated unity. In a family the agreement of thought and action in its members hardly forms an integrated unity. The same thing is true of larger groups. By the group mind is meant that in the group many have common interests and activities. Groups are organized to a degree but only to a degree.

And the rationalistic idealism, despite its claim of being an all-inclusive philosophy, eliminates from its world some significant aspects of human experience—novelty, spontaneitiy, creativity, and genuine freedom, as emphasized by philosophers like Bergson, James, Dewey, and Whitehead. These aspects are sacrificed to establish a logical, necessitarian system. Not that they are ignored by the rationalists, but their meaning and vitality are compromised to fit them into a strict internally related logical system. One must admit the importance of deterministic or causal demands, but one must equally insist on the importance of the artist's demand for creativity, and of the moralist's demand for genuine free choice. Blanshard introduces the notion of degrees of causality to alleviate the sting of moral determinism, but this notion is too obscure to meet the issue.

Finally, as to the pragmatic value of such a system. Idealism was described above as the philosophy of aspiration and hope, and as the interpretation of reality in terms of the higher cagetories of mind and spirit. Individuals who wish to find in the rationalistic idealism of Blanshard a philosophy akin to a religious outlook that would sustain their wishes with a basic cosmic support will be disappointed. Blanshard's final system or the Whole is not in any sense akin to mind as we actually know it but only to the impersonal sense of reason. His system in many resepcts is akin to the world of mechanism rather than to that of spiritualism in the usual religious sense. Logical necessity replaces the active integrating conception of mind. The Whole assumes the form of a self-sufficient logical system, and is really an impersonal system, "without a live Thinker". This aspect of rationalistic idealism has been emphasized not because it was thought that a philosophic system should satisfy human hopes, but because what should be pointed out is the considerable transformation of recent idealism from the earlier spiritualistic forms.

As there is no sufficient evidence that the universe is a tight rational-istic system, one can live without accepting such a belief. An extreme form of rationalism has no practical bearing whatsoever. One may claim that everything one does is completely determined by the Whole, but as long as the Whole is beyond our knowledge our decisions are relevant and limited to the immediate finite setting.

And yet rationalistic idealism has made some important contributions. The notions of reason, system, and context of meaning need to be pointed out. Even the extreme empiricists must introduce in some form or other the function of reason; the pluralists cannot completely forego the unifying relevance of system; and the analysts of meaning will find the notion of contextual meaning fruitful. The criticisms of the present discussion are not directed against these central concepts but against the indefensible exaggerations of these concepts by the rationalistic idealists.

VII

THE PHILOSOPHY OF ALFRED NORTH WHITEHEAD

In the modern era there have been many penetrating philosophic analyses of specific. well-defined areas—of science, politics, morals and art—but bold, sweeping systems, such as give a broad synthesis of reality and are generally meant when we speak of metaphysics, have been rare. One reason for this scarcity has been the reaction against the grandiose, dogmatic systems of the past; another has been the contemporary positivistic temper of mind that tends to limit philosophic claims to observable statements; and still a third has been the realization that the task of metaphysics, if it is to be done in a responsible manner, is infinitely difficult. Alfred North Whitehead is one of the few exceptions. He has constructed a metaphysics that is at once spacious, coherent and undogmatic—one that has integrated the latest developments of science with other rich phases of human experience.

This metaphysics is the result of a lifetime of activity and reflection in a number of fields. In his earlier years Whitehead was a mathematician at Cambridge University and later at the University of London. His *A Treatise on Universal Algebra* and the monumental three-volume *Principia Mathematica*, written in collaboration with Bertrand Russell, belong to that period. But even this early in his career Whitehead's interest was more philosophical than mathematical. He was concerned with basic, general ideas of mathematics rather than with specific mathematical problems. He next became interested in the physical sciences. His books, *An Enquiry Concerning the Principles of Natural Knowledge, The Concept of Nature and The Principle of Relativity*, belong together and here again his concern was definitely philosophical. In these books he was already beginning to propound a new type of natural philosophy. Finally, when in 1924 he was invited to a professorship in philosophy by Harvard University, where he taught until his retirement in 1937, he developed his metaphysics in detail. The full and final account of his philosophic system is given in his trilogy : *Science and the Modern World*, an exciting book which contains a sketch of his metaphysics; *Process and Reality*, his magnum opus; and *Adventures of Ideas*, the most readable of his books.

PART I

Whitehead has left a deep impression on contemporary thought. What, then are his key ideas?,

First, as for Whitehead's approach to his task as philosopher. In his own words, speculative philosophy is "the endeavor to frame a coherent, logical, necessary system of general ideas in terms of which every element of our experience can be interpreted".[1] In this definition both reason and experience have their place. Whitehead is thus a rationalist as well as an empiricist.

The key idea in Whitehead's interpretation of reality is process, and the title of his major work reminds us of this fact. The notion of process was eloquently expressed in early Greek philosophy by Heraclitus: "You cannot step twice into the same river; for fresh waters are ever flowing in upon us". In modern philosophy Bergson, James, Dewey, and Alexander have again made change or flux the central concept of philosophy. The transitoriness of everyday events, the principle of evolution, and the recent theories of matter all favor such a view.

Whitehead's notion of process is rich and many-sided. First, process is a universal happening in the spatio-temporal world. Every point in nature is in the throes of change—some swifter, others slower. There are no permanent substances, no immutable material particles, no self-sufficient realities. In Whitehead's view "becoming" attains greater importance metaphysically than "being". As he expresses it, "The world is always becoming, and as it becomes it passes away and perishes". Second, world-process or becoming is not sheer flux, formless continuity, but is atomized, individualized into units of process. Passing events initiate new processes. The creative activity of emerging events brings together various elements of the prior events to form new syntheses that are characterized by new qualities and activities. In time these new syntheses disintegrate and become

---

[1] *Process and Reality* (New York : Macmillan Co., 1929), p. 4.

material for future events. This pattern of world-process is endless. Whitehead calls the units of process "actual entities". These are the ultimate facts of reality; there is no going behind them to anything more real. These units are not observable objects like stones, trees, or human beings; they are too microscopic and transitory. They are like a vibration or pulse; yet every object is nothing more than a complex grouping of these processes. Finally, a given process, and this is the most controversial aspect of Whitehead's suggestion, is not merely a physical event but rather a center or pulse of experience. Individualized processes are, if you like, miniatures of human experience. They have feelings and are guided by aims. Even atoms and molecules, for Whitehead, are composed of processes which possess inner experience. Thus nature is alive at every point. This does not mean that every process has "conscious" experience, but it does mean that all processes have experience in the widest sense of the term. Whitehead's metaphysics becomes essentially a type of panpsychism.

In the turmoil of the changing world there is still, for Whitehead, something permanent. All passing and perishing events exhibit certain qualities that are not exposed to the ravages of time. Fallen leaves that are carried away by the winds, joyous moods that are changed by succeeding events, have eternal characteristics. The same shade of green or the same oval contour observed in one of the drifting leaves may recur in the future; the same joyous mood may recur. Qualities like greenness, ovalness, joyfulness, usually designated "universals", Whitehead calls "eternal objects". Eternal objects, for him, do not emerge from nature to perish like other events—they invade nature, or "ingress" (to use his own term) into the events of nature.

Whitehead's thought here, with some modifications, is similar to Plato's. Plato, in his attempt to reconcile the conflict between the changing and the changeless, the temporal and the eternal, had suggested the theory of Ideas or Forms. What one perceives, he claimed, are imperfect, perishing copies of immutable, eternal models. All straight lines, for example, as perceived by the senses are only crude repetitions of an ideal straight line. Similarly, Whitehead's eternal objects are immutable. They are not confined to the spatio-temporal world, yet they may be exemplified in the transitory events of this world. But Whitehead's eternal objects, unlike Plato's Ideas, are not superior realities; they are, rather, possibilities of realization.

One further question : How does one explain the fact that eternal objects as possibilities are actualized in the world in a rational, orderly way? The world exhibits a rational order, yet it might have been a chaos. Events occur as if prescribed by certain standards, yet they might have been altogether capricious. Whitehead thinks reality must contain some principle of limitation or selection to make this orderliness possible. This principle of limitation or rationality he calls "God". One may wish to ask, "Why should there be this principle or rationality, this God?" No answer can be given to this question, since God as the principle of rationality is the ground for the presence of everything. Not even God can account for His presence.

Yet Whitehead's God is not merely a metaphysical principle, but an object to satisfy religious aspiration. His god is persuasive rather than coercive; not omnipotent, but a "fellow-sufferer who understands". He is "wisdom". He is the poet of the world "with tender patience leading it by his vision of truth, beauty, and goodness".[2]

Whitehead's metaphysics is one of the most daring and magnificent philosophical creations of our time. As against the abstractions of nineteenth-century scientific materialism he emphasizes concreteness and fidelity to experience. As against the irresponsible speculation of romanticists he insists on the necessity of incorporating into one's philosophy matters of fact and the most exacting recent theories of science. As against many thin current philosophies he richly weaves together various aspects of experience; change with permanence, causality with teleology, science with religion, modern hopes with traditional values. Nevertheless there are serious objections to Whitehead's philosophy.

In his speculative philosophy he presents the types of claim that are denied to empirical knowledge. It is true that he is scrupulously empirical whenever the matter under discussion permits; yet in his attempt to fill the gaps in our consciousness he suggests ideas which are basically not verifiable. In this respect he partly revives the classic role of philosophy as something having access to knowledge which is not open to the uninitiated. But this role seems doubtful to many. Whitehead rightly points out that a true metaphysics must do justice to all phases of experience and that one's final interpretation of reality must escape the abstractions of the specific sciences; yet to achieve such an all-embracing philosophy it should not be necessary to go beyond natural, experimental knowledge. What we need is a more empirical metaphysics than Whitehead has offered.

[2] *Ibid.*, p. 526.

Take Whitehead's basic contention that every process, even the physical one, involves inner experience; that every point in the universe has feeling and is guided by a subjective aim. This affirmation is certainly not the result of empirical knowledge. On the contrary, it is nothing more than a postulate which goes beyond inductive knowledge to satisfy the demands of concreteness and of the continuity of matter and mind. And though one must make serious attempts to meet these demands, one's procedure must not, like Whitehead's introduce greater difficulties than one started with.

Similarly unwarranted is his claim that reality must contain a principle of limitation, by him called God, as a ground for the actualization of possibilities. Unless one adheres to Whitehead's theories of eternal objects and actual entities, which are highly controversial, there is no need of going outside of nature to make sense of natural happenings. It is true that Whitehead's metaphysical God is free from most of the obscurities of the traditional gods. But one cannot help pointing out that this postulate gets one involved in the same difficulties as characterize every non-empirical philosophy.

Whitehead's metaphysics is an impressive alternative to naturalistic philosophy. To some his philosophy may be a new source of hope for retaining beliefs which have been deeply disturbed by science; but to others his occasional flights beyond the natural world are invitations they cannot accept. Yet even the latter need not deprive themselves of Whitehead's rich and generous insights.

PART II

The transition from Whitehead's metaphysics to his philosophy of civilization is a natural one. Since every throb of existence has value, one must appreciate the unique value of each human being.

First, as to the nature of a civilized society. Whitehead developed his idea of civilization primarily in his *Adventures of Ideas*, and in some of his essays on social philosophy. The notion of civilization is a complex and ambiguous one. Though Whitehead fully realizes the difficulties involved, he would like civilization to mean a society that makes possible a meaningful and enjoyable life for all. Historically, civilization for Whitehead is the victory of persuasion over force. Civilization is the maintenance "of social order by its own inherent persuasiveness as embodying the nobler alternative".[3] Resort to

---

[3] *Adventure of Ideas* (New York : Macmillan & Co., 1933), p. 105.

force is a sign of the failure of civilization. The great idea which Plato gave to the world, and which was further developed by Christianity, was that the divine element in the world is not the coercive but the persuasive one .This humanitarian ideal developed the notion of the dignity of man and undermined the early prevalent idea of slavery. And this humanitarian ideal has increased the sensitivity to human possibilities. For Whitehead these possibilities are truth, beauty, adventure, art, and peace. A civilized society is one that exhibits these values in all the phases of its activity. He analyzes these concepts in detail. Beauty, for example, is patterned contrast. Adventure is the search for perfection and not mere geographical exploration. As static perfection is not possible, the only choice is progress or decadence. Without adventure civilization is bound to decay. Peace is not mere absence of strife—industrial or international—but immunity to the distractions of existence. It is obtained by devotion to exalted ideals and by steady reliance on the efficacy of noble actions.

Civilization is not, as often assumed, a mere knowledge or imitation of the best of the past; it involves freshness and novelty. As Whitehead puts it, "A race preserves its vigor so long as it harbours a real contrast between what has been and what may be; and so long as it is nerved by the vigor of adventure beyond the safeties of the past. Without adventure civilization is in full decay".[4] Values of civilization, for Whitehead, are not mere abstractions but the actual experiences of individuals. Civilization is characterized by the maximum respect for individuals.

The ideal society can never be realized, only approximated. Whitehead's very notion of reality as process makes all accomplishment provisional. Yet he is basically optimistic. He suggests some major conditions that make possible a high degree of civilization.

One of these conditions is the prevalence of more humane ideas. "As we think we live".[5] In each era there are some ideas which are so pervasive that they are accepted like the air we breathe. In the Hellenistic-Roman period the idea of slavery was taken to be inescapable. Yet more humane ideas of man ushered in the primacy of the ideas of freedom and equality. Whitehead, of course, in his emphasis on the efficacy of ideas does not ignore the importance of custom. Ideas to be effective must be "massively coordinated inheritance".

---

[4] *Ibid.*, p. 360.
[5] *Modes of Thought*, (New York, Macmillan & Co., 1938), p. 87.

Another condition that makes for civilization is an economic system that harmonizes with the cultural needs of the individual. Whitehead especially emphasizes this condition. The fusion of the ideal with the economic policies makes" the stuff of history".[6] In our present economic system there is "a starvation of human impulses, a denial of opportunity, a limitation of beneficial activity—in short, a lack of freedom".[7] Whitehead makes some suggestions in the direction of improvement: greater employer-employee cooperation, more creative work, beautiful surroundings for industrial plants.

Finally, more vitally motivated education can make an important contribution to civilization. Whitehead was a distinguished educator and had a rich experience in some of the leading universities. Education must not deal exclusively with abstract intellectual concepts and factual knowledge. "A merely well-informed man is the most useless bore on God's earth". Abstract or factual knowledge is useful only when it promotes worthy thought and action. At many points Whitehead's and Dewey's views on education are strikingly similar. Most of what Whitehead writes on civilization is challenging; yet some of his suggestions involve difficulties.

First, to what extent do ideas determine history? This is a difficult issue. Ideas have an important role in history; and at a time when many anti-intellectual movements depreciate their significance, one should be reminded of their efficacy. Yet to what degree are they effective? Was the abolition of slavery primarily due to democracy or to the fact that it was uneconomical under technological conditions? Many would give the main weight to these conditions. Whitehead is not unaware of such situations; yet when he writes, "... it was democracy that freed the slaves", or when he says, "As we think we live", one feels he tends to give too sweeping a power to ideas. Often it is truer to say,"As we live we think".

Whitehead's suggestions on the present economic system fall mostly in the efficiency-building area, though he is not so much interested in efficiency as in the development of more humane and cultured industrial relations. The suggestions are fruitful as far as they go, but he fails to consider the tougher and more basic economic issues, such as the fair distribution of wealth and the more democratic

---

[6] *Adventure of Ideas*, p. 88.

[7] *Whitehead's American Essays in Social Philosophy*, Edited by A. H. Johnson, (New York, Harper and Brothers, Publishers, 1956), p. 76.

control of economic forces, without consideration of which his suggestions would not much alter the present situation.

As for Whitehead's views on persuasion, which are so central to his whole view of civilization, one can fully agree with his espousal of this method as the only civilized way of settling conflicts, and can approve his eloquent defense of it. But can society wholly dispense with force? Men seem to be pretty generally convinced that sometimes force is the only means that is left for reaching decisions. When a deadlock occurs between conflicting aims, there is nothing left but to fight it out. Though force is not a substitute for reason in human affairs, it might well be an element in the rational life.

Whether one agrees or not with Whitehead's specific suggestions for improving our society, one is exposed, while reading his discussions on civilization, to a mind that is genuinely humanistic, deeply concerned with the achievement of an imaginatively rich civilization; and one is also enlivened by the essential optimism of this mind that yet does not ignore the complexities that lie across the path toward the ideal society. I wish myself that he had explored more adequately the darker aspects of our society. But if courage and hope are prerequisites for success in our pursuit of an ideal society, then Whitehead's rational optimism remains of great value.

VIII

SHELDON'S SYNTHETIC METAPHYSICS

Wilmon Sheldon has known better than most contemporary philosophers the art of surveying reality from an inclusive point of view. In a number of previous valuable volumes he has argued for a synthetic metaphysics which finds its full expression in his recent major work, *God and Polarity*.[1] Sheldon's thesis is that metaphysical systems "are in the main correct—except when they think they have refuted the others. It may be that if the onlooker would dig beneath the surface, he would see that the quarrels are needless, that each type of metaphysics *has* shown its truth—though not always in the way it supposes—that the warring factions *can* pool their results without any being relegated to inferior grade".[2] As long as philosophers continue their exclusive love and mutual refutations, their quest "cannot command the respect of earnest souls who have the good of humanity deeply at heart; nor does it deserve the same".[3] Philosophers must set their house in order. United "they may stand, divided they *must* fall".[4] Sheldon in developing this high purpose presents one of the most impressive contemporary metaphysical systems. It is rich in insights and vast in scope. I shall first state his metaphysics in large outline, and then estimate some of his basic ideas.

I

In his enterprise to develop a synthetic metaphysics Sheldon first attempts to determine the criterion of reality, What is the test

---

[1] *God and Polarity: A Synthesis of Philosophies.* (New Haven: Yale University Press; London : Oxford University Press, 1954), 712 pp.

[2] *Ibid.*, p. 3.

[3] *Ibid.*, p. 3.

[4] *Ibid.*, p. 3.

or procedure that will get at the external reality? Modern philosophy, according to him, has created an impasse through its intense epistemological interest, an interest he considers unnatural. Pure contemplation of reality, mere analysis of sensations, and, more recently, the extreme analytic procedure of analysis have drawn us farther and farther away from reality and have closed us within a subjective world. These procedures, Sheldon argues, never reach the external wold : contemplation cannot go beyond thought; analysis of sensation cannot go beyond the experience of sensation; and the latest analysts even regard such terms as *reality, independent, external world* as relics of the Dark Ages. How shall we escape the present predicament?

Sheldon makes the fruitful suggestion that in action, as against mere thought or sensation, one is able to escape the subjectivism of the modern epistemologists. In his words, "Action plays the part of dooropener to the outer world of reality".[5] Reality is directly conveyed by action. Seeing is believing, but acting is proving, proving not by reasoning as epistemologists would insist, but by direct experience. The test of reality is not from without, but from within action itself. For common sense this is ultimate.

More specifically, action or effort, for Sheldon, is, first of all, always purposive : it always involves some idea, however dim or ambiguous, of what it desires. It is strife for something we want : "to have the car move, to raise the stone, to see the problem's answer, to behave reasonably, to be quiet".[6] Secondly, action is originative. "The unique positive thing about effort is its originality; ... it is ... not a datum but a factum, or better still, a fiat, a doing rather than a deed".[7] It is in the initiative of a process. Thirdly, action is out-goingness. Action moves away from its own being to the object. Thus its direction is opposite to that of thought. Thought carries meaning inward to the mind; action goes outward to the object. Thought is still, immanent; action is dynamic, transitive, This out-goingness is what gives to action its incalculable import. Finally, action is self-effacing, transparent; being increasingly submerged in the object, it is able to witness an independent reality. When slipping down the bank into a lake— to use Sheldon's illustration—one casts about frantically for a hand-

[5] *Ibid.*, p. 23.
[6] *Ibid.*, p. 28.
[7] *Ibid.*, p. 30.

hold. One's consciousness is filled with the object—the slippery slope, the lake, the needed holdfast—and not with awareness of what the nature of the experience is.

Yet Sheldon, with his synthetic spirit, gives consideration to other aspects of mind in our attempt to reach external reality. Cognition and affection have equally valuable functions in human knowledge. Though action is prior, it is not superior to other phases of mind. Cognition (thought and sensation) gives content to action, adds the *what* to the *that* of action; it formulates hypotheses for the guidance of action; it examines the relation of possibles to actuals; it brings order and coherence to experience. Thus cognition, over and above the action test, brings the coherence-test to knowledge. Action and thought are polar but not opposing powers of mind. The two cooperate on the same level : "In the world they are always together. No mere power, no mere order anywhere in reality. Reality is rational as being orderly; also it has extrarational factors in the midst of its order".[8] The two are "opposites, not opposed, but counterparts like the poles of a magnet except for the compulsory implication between the magnetic poles".[9]

And these two phases of mind are united in affection. Thought does not compel action. What brings together or induces cooperation between the possible ideals of thought and the doings of action is affection. Sheldon uses Whitehead's favorite term "lure". Lure works by drawing, not by pushing or forcing. The lure "is the final not the efficient cause; the power of the efficient cause is compelling, of the final is the good that lures by its goodness".[10] And we all act on the external world as long as we are alive and have desires to fulfill. Without a lure a man would not act; even though lure does not compel the decision, there would be no decision, no motive to adopt, without it. Yet lure that unites thought and action also promotes each in its singularity".[11] We love action for action's sake, and thinking for thought's sake.

To the active-cognitive-affective process Sheldon gives the name "experiment" or "experimental testing". Experiment involves action, thought, and the desire to know. The criterion of reality "is given by

[8] *Ibid.*, p. 111.
[9] *Ibid.*, p. 111.
[10] *Ibid.*, p. 114.
[11] *Ibid.*, p. 121.

action, by experiment".[12] And, again, *"reason alone never convinces in respect of reality.* Experimental verification *after* or *with* reasoning *does* convince".[13] "Proof in respect of real things is experimental; it is never *merely* logical".[14]

Sheldon's approach to reality makes clear his interpretation of the nature of reality. First, and foremost, reality is power; it is what resists our efforts. As he expresses it in one of his earlier books, "Reality is primarily that power or those powers which we find we have to respect when we act to gain the ends we need".[15] Or, as stated more succinctly in the present book, "Power is being and being is power".[16] Secondly, reality is order, coherence, though this order need not ignore the chance element in nature. So, for Sheldon "reality is" to a degree "diffuse, indeterminate. Probability rather than *strict* causality governs the minute details of nature. Probability applies to the group and leaves the individual event indeterminate within limits".[17] Finally, reality is value, value in the sense that whatever is real "is good or bad so far as it fulfills or frustrates wants or innate trends, whether of itself or other things".[18] Thus, in final description, "Reality ... is power, order, and value".[19]

Having prepared the ground for the approach to reality, Sheldon surveys the enduring metaphysical systems and through his experimental method determines their insights. This section, which forms the major part of the book, is an invaluable contribution to current philosophy. Major philosophic systems are analyzed thoroughly, critically, and at the same time generously—a procedure quite different from that of the current refutationists. The analysis of different schools is primarily philosophical rather than historical. And what is also significant is that each philosophical system is placed within its larger, world setting. Indian and Chinese philosophic ideas find adequate expression in his discussion. Yet despite his basically synthetic attitude, certain schools, such as Thomism for instance, are

---

[12] *Ibid.*, p. 80.

[13] *Ibid.*, p. 81.

[14] *Ibid.*, pp. 222-223.

[15] *America's Progressive Philosophy* (New Haven : Yale University Press, 1942), p. 96.

[16] God and Polarity, p. 38.

[17] *Ibid.*, p. 105.

[18] *Ibid.*, p. 123.

[19] *Ibid.*, p. 123.

analyzed with deep affection, whereas others, like materialism and contemporary analysis, are rather harshly treated. Of these two systems he can hardly be said to have presented the inner élan. Should not his principle of polarity have led him to do greater justice to the analysts for instance, whose school he should have regarded as being the opposite of, rather than opposing, the school of synthetic philosophy?

Sheldon's survey of systems arrives at the following grand result. Monistic idealism proves the existence of a Supreme Spirit, "perfect so far as man can see, source of utmost bliss. The proof is given in the mystical experiment".[20] Even when "the idealists did not perform the experiment but relied only on a rational argument ... that argument irrespective of its soundness has been verified by the experiment".[21] Pluralistic idealism proves the ultimate reality of conscious personal minds from "the fact that we have to conduct our lives by accepting that reality".[22] Materialism rightly affirms that material beings are ultimate, irreducible to mental terms. We all have to adapt ourselves to physical nature if we are to live. Thomism, a truly synthetic system for Sheldon, assimilates the truths of idealism and materialism. And in addition to its doctrine of Divine existence it asserts the levels of being. It also asserts such pairs as essence and existence, substance and accident, act and potency. Process-philosophy emphasizes the import of time and emergentism as opening the door to higher values. Existentialism asserts the extrarational or irrational in existence and in the conative-affective aspect of mind.

Having stated the positive insights of the major metaphysical systems, Sheldon has now to weave these insights into an original synthetic system of his own. He accomplishes this task through the principles of polarity and grades of being. The first principle concerns primarily the particular things themselves, while the second concerns primarily the general spread of things in a sort of hierarchy.

First, the principle of polarity. For Sheldon polarity is the most pervasive specific trait of reality. He gives the following definition of polarity : "One or another phase, aspect, relation, event or entity and its counterpart, each peculiar to the other alone, *its* counterpart; the two opposite as it were in direction, in way of acting, yet each capable of fruitful cooperation with the other, also of opposing, denying or

---

[20] *Ibid.*, p. 667.
[21] *Ibid.*, p. 667.
[22] *Ibid.*, p. 668.

frustrating it, having thus a degree of independence and a being of its own, and between the two a trend or lure to cooperation in which one of the partners takes the initiative and the other responds, yet each freely; the relation has a certain asymmetry".[23] Time-space, essence-existence, actual-possible, structure-process, cause-chance, inorganic-organic, body-mind, male-female, value-fact are illustrations of polarity.

Second, the principle of grades of being. This principle is based on that of plenitude. Sheldon finds a tendency in nature to realize all possibles and also a drift to go from the simplest to the most inclusive beings, each "including the powers of the level next below yet adding a new contribution of its own not quite reducible to terms of the other".[24] Being has degrees, but not being just as existence, but existence realizing potencies, essences, which may be distinguished as greater or smaller. So "degree of being is degree of value".[25] God is the Supreme Being, in whom essence and existence are at their fullest. And for Sheldon the existence of God is certain on the basis of the First Cause Argument, though to this argument he adds his own subtle ontological argument. He also considers the mystical experience as an experimental proof of the existence of God.

Sheldon takes insights from all the great historic and contemporary systems. His theism is Thomistic; his theory of levels of being and, up to a point, his theory of the organic unity of reality are Hegelian; his defense of body and mind is dualistic; his attitude toward chance as well as toward causality is pluralistic; his insistence on time and emergence brings him close to process-philosophy; his insistence on the extrarational is existential. All these ideas are woven into an impressive and original synthetic philosophy.

II

Now that I have given a description of Sheldon's metaphysics, I shall examine some of his key ideas : his methodology, his theories of reality, polarity, and grades of being, and his conception of synthesis.

1. *Method.* Despite Sheldon's sharp comments on the methodol-

---

[23] *Ibid.*, p. 674.
[24] *Ibid.*, p. 702.
[25] *Ibid.*, p. 703.

ogists, he himself gives considerable attention to ways of knowing reality and offers fruitful suggestions on this subject. For him, as earlier mentioned, action opens the door to reality, and cognition and affection also play a role in the final construction of knowledge. It is the joint operation of the three that for him constitutes experimentalism. It would not be incorrect to say that he advocates experimentalism as the most adequate method in our pursuit of knowledge. In this connection he frequently mentions his affinity to the pragmatists and especially to Dewey. And while reading his book one becomes aware not only of private, inaccessible experiences, which he so strongly emphasizes, but even more of an outdoor reality and varied human activities. I presume Sheldon would like to be called an extrovert rather than an introvert philosopher. And to a high degree he is. In discussing his theory of method I shall refer to two issues : the relation of action to external reality, and the applicability of experimentalism to various specific areas of reality.

(a) The first question to be considered is : Does Sheldon's method break the epistemological impasse, which he so vividly describes, and give us the external world without any modification, that is, as it is, the thing in itself? His approach to this problem in terms of action is most fruitful. Of course, as epistemological difficulties crowd in upon him in the form of experiences of error, dream and illusion, he dismisses them with a fiat by maintaining that reality is directly given by action. Action is proving, by direct experience. For him there is no criterion for the reality of the external world from without, the test is found within action itself. Accepting his approach to this problem as a fruitful one, the one issue I wish to raise is : Is action ever so transparent, so self-effacing, so submerged in the external object as to give the independent reality directly, untainted by any modification? This claim he fails to establish fully.

In every type of action, as Sheldon himself suggests, thought comes into the picture. The *that* of action is clothed, interpreted, and classified in terms of the *what* of thought. It is true that we can distinguish between so-called hard, independent facts of reality and the classification to which we subject them; yet these very facts are themselves partly the resultant of prior classification. At no stage of our endless pursuit of knowledge of reality are we ever free of choosing some mode of interpretation; and our series of choices is involved in what we may ultimately mean by reality. Strictly our knowledge is *about facts* rather than *of fact*. To say, therefore, as Sheldon does, that through action we can reach "things as they are themselves" is not what the experimentalist tells us. Rather, reality, facts, or "things in themselves" are ideals, in the sense that they are the ideal limits in our endless process of approximation to truth; and the distinction between appearance and reality is the distinction between the less and the more real.

(b) The second question that needs consideration is : To what extent does Sheldon apply the experimental method—which he claims he does—to establish his specific philosophic claims? On this issue his procedure raises several doubts, since he uses the experimental method in a somewhat Pickwickian way. Sometimes experimentalism is given such a wide meaning that its applicability tends to become irresponsible; at other times the consequences of experimental procedure are refused; and at still other times attempts are made to establish existential claims by the method of pure rationalism, despite the fact that he so vigorously and rightly criticizes this procedure.

To exemplify his too wide meaning of experimentalism : "Monist idealism has proved the existence of a Supreme Spirit, perfect so far as man can see, source of utmost bliss. The proof is given in the mystical experiment".[26] And if one asks in what way mysticism proves this claim, his answer is : "Look at the results : that is the answer". That the mystic experiences bliss may be unshakable. From this fact Sheldon draws the conclusion that the mystic's assertions about the Supreme Spirit are true. But is not Sheldon too closely identifying the mystics' actual experience with the latter's interpretation of this experience? Mysticism is certainly open to a more empirical interpretation, that is, in terms of values within the verifiable setting of human nature, human culture, and nature. Sheldon's frequent attempt to identify experimentalism with beliefs that have beneficial consequences makes experimentalism an unmanageable procedure. If experimentalism is to be a responsible procedure, it must deal with publicly verifiable hypotheses.

And let us turn now to Sheldon's refusal to accept the consequences of experimental procedure in relation to certain issues in spite of his insistence that he is adhering to experimentalism. In dealing with the problem of knowledge of other minds, he offers us these heartening words : "... the certainty of other minds is to be guaranteed in the same experimental or practical way as is the certainty of the external

---

[26] *Ibid.*, p. 660.

physical world".[27] But feeling somewhat uneasy about the consequences of this procedure, he immediately adds to this statement : "with a difference added, yes, but a difference only in the manner and motive of the experiment".[28] What, then, is the nature of other minds? Other minds are "private, hidden" experiences. All we can do is go around them. The analogy Sheldon uses is that other minds are like the vacuole in the continuous protoplasm of a living cell : a hole indeed that cannot be crossed, but that nevertheless can be gone around. If other minds are to be determined experimentally, why resort to procedures which are by definition inaccessible to private realms? What is open to verification is behavior, so that if one is to take the experimental procedure seriously, why not say that mind is behavior? A thing is what it does. One need not deny the private aspect of other minds, nor need this be inaccessible forever, since it should become increasingly open to empirical investigation.

Finally, there is Sheldon's resort to pure rationalism in establishing existential propositions. Though he approves what he calls experimental verification of the existence of God in terms of mystical experience, he also revives the ontological argument. Though, rather ingeniously, he formulates the ontological argument in more objective terms than usual, yet in the end he derives God from His essence. As Sheldon puts it : "... God Himself is the necessary being. Which means that His being *can* be accounted for, deduced; His very nature makes Him exist".[29] If Sheldon admits that deductive arguments can prove existential truths, why should he be so critical, as he rightly is, of the rationalistic tradition?

2. *Reality.* Being primarily a metaphysician, Sheldon is interested in methodology because it enables him to make a map of reality and to formulate principles that can guide one in life. He has found that reality has three general traits : power, coherence, and value.

Power, for him, is the primary trait of reality. It is possible for coherence and value to be in the realm of pure possibles without being actuals. There are different modes of power : physical, vital, mental, and divine. The first thing to be noted is that his notion of power does not imply universal "anthropomorphism". It is true that sometimes we meet resistance from other wills than our own,

[27] *Ibid.*, p. 127.
[28] *Ibid.*, p. 127.
[29] *Ibid.*, p. 527.

but, as Sheldon points out, there is nothing in the resistance offered by physical objects to suggest that they have feelings, still less conscious purposes. Secondly, his notion of power does not hypostatize power as an agency over and above process or action itself. Reality as power means resistance, process, action, doing something. A thing is what it does, and one might add, what it can potentially do.

The notion of power as doing something applies to everything. In Sheldon's words : "A man is what he does. His worth lies in what he makes. ... so we all believe when we conduct our lives in intercourse with one another and with nature".[30] Does Sheldon follow the consequences of his notion of power as a definition of reality? Not always. If he had done so, his philosophy whould have been much nearer to a naturalistic process-philosophy, like Dewey's, without the body-mind and nature-supernature dualisms. Applying Sheldon's definition of reality as power one should say : Matter is that testable process which makes one call things physical; life is that testable activity which makes one call it living. These different modes of reality are different modes of testable power. There is, therefore, no necessity when describing mind or nature, as Sheldon does, to assume something over and above action or behavior. Mind is what mind does; it is behavior, or rather a specific type of behavior. Nature is what nature does; there is no need of referring to some supreme agency or a First Cause to explain nature.

Reality is, also, coherence, up to a point. Sheldon as synthetic metaphysician wants to do justice to order and contingency, to causality and chance in nature. He maintains that in order to live, to carry out our plans, we must have a belief in the uniformity of nature, and that in order to realize our ideals of progress and morals we must have a belief in chance, not chance in the negative sense as the mere denial of causal necessity but chance in the positive sense that all possibles tend to be actualized. How shall we reconcile these two demands? Sheldon suggests that the statistical view of the laws of nature reconciles these two demands : it provides sufficient uniformity and sufficient opportunity for chance. This view is appealing and many contemporary distinguished scientists and philosophers argue for a somewhat similar view. Especially in the light of recent developments in physics, such as quantum mechanics, the statistical view of the laws of nature has attained wide acceptance. The issues involved

---

[30] *Ibid.*, p. 31.

here are too intricate to be analyzed in passing. Yet one may offer the suggestion that the scientist's demand for an increasingly deterministic image of nature and the moralist's demand for a view of nature that increasingly allows genuine possibility and freedom need not be incompatible. For certain purposes the events of experience may be classified in a deterministic way, for other purposes in a statistical way. The issue, as Sheldon rightly argues, is an empirical one, but one has to pursue one's empirical investigations in the light of certain demands or ideals. And the demand for more and more precision is an abiding ideal of science.

Finally, reality is value. One certainly cannot disagree with Sheldon when he claims that reality is the source of our desires, hopes, and aspirations. In this sense one may speak of reality as value. (Sheldon. of course, equally emphasizes the relation of possibilities to value; as he puts it, "Possibles make progress possible".) But Sheldon's claim about reality as value goes further. For him, anything that fulfills its potency has intrinsic value. "Efficient and final cause both hold of each and every event throughout nature, so far as the event succeeds in realizing its latent trends or potencies".[31] The using of concepts like function, purpose, final cause, and teleology is practicable in relation to artifacts, instruments, living beings, human beings, and social groups; but using them in relation to the physical world tends to make them lose their distinctive meaning. A panpsychist may appropriately apply such teleological concepts to the physical world, but Sheldon is not a panpsychist, in fact he presents one of the most devastating criticisms of panpsychism in current philosophy. His usage is Thomistic, and Thomism is open to the same kind of criticism.

3. *Polarity*. Sheldon makes much use of the principle of polarity. It is the most original phase of his philosophy. First presented in his book *Strife of Systems* in 1918, this principle has attained greater clarity and fuller expression in the present book.

The principle of polarity has four major traits : the relation of opposites; the trend or lure toward cooperation of opposites; the degree of independence of opposites; and the relation of asymmetry between opposites. The principle of polarity may apply to a single individual or between individuals; in the latter case between an individual of a class and another of a counterpart class or between two individuals of independent classes. The following are illustrations of the

---

[31] *Ibid.*, p. 687.

polarity principle : the right hand and the left hand, male and female, essence and existence, efficient cause and final cause, the material absorbed by plants and its formation into structure, the nucleus and the cytoplasm of cells, and mind and body in man.

The polarity principle, for Sheldon, is primarily ontological. "The pairing principle ... pervades reality ... it is practically ubiquitous. ... it seems to be the most pervasive specific trait in nature; specific as having a unique definable character, distinguishable, identifiable in the concrete".[32] Polarity is also a normative principle. "Polarity furnishes the key to the settlement of the great perennial quarrels of types".[33] Polarity lets each type say, "I am right in and by myself, so are you my opposite. ... Let us then gladly recognize the truth of each other and cooperate to gain a broader ... view". I shall consider these two aspects of the polarity principle.

First, as an ontological principle. Whether the polarity principle applies to nature is primarily an empirical question. The events of experience may be classified in many different ways : quantitatively, qualitatively, causally, teleologically, as opposites, as opposed, and so on. The central question in all these various types of classification is : How fruitful or pragmatically justifiable is a given classification in relation to the problem or purpose involved? The polarity principle provides us with the possibility of doing justice to identity and difference, to causality and teleology, to matter and mind, to unity and plurality. It also helps one to approach and formulate certain significant problems in biology, psychology, and the social sciences. Sheldon's polarity principle is much more fertile and concrete than most of his critics have granted. Yet despite these advantages one cannot say that the polarity principle has the predictive power of causal, statistical, or teleological explanations. And for Sheldon, and rightly so, it is power that counts in the end. In terms of consequences polarity does not seem to have the cosmic significance that he attributes to it.

And again, it may be noted that the principle of polarity does not *necessarily* establish Sheldon's basically dualistic metaphysics. A naturalist, and especially the non-reductive type of naturalist, could equally and as fruitfully use the principle of polarity without admitting a deep, dualistic cleavage in reality. Mind and body, for exam-

[32] *Ibid.*, p. 674.
[33] *Ibid.*, p. 677.

ple, are opposites, yet they need not differ in the sense of the dualistic metaphysican but merely as kinds of behavior. The polarity principle is neutral as far as most metaphysical systems are concerned.

By way of analogy one may cite the situation in the second decade of this century when the neo-realists tried to establish some of their ontological doctrines by using the notions of simple terms, asymmetrical relations, and the infinite continuum of symbolic logic. Because at that time most philosophers were ignorant of symbolic logic, the arguments of the neo-realists sounded impressive and seemed final. Yet it became obvious in time that the categories of symbolic logic, like the categories of calculus, were neutral to metaphysical systems. Or, to put it another way, any metaphysical system could make use of them. Certainly Sheldon makes effective use of the principle of polarity for his synthetic metaphysics, but the door is open to others to make similar use of it for their metaphysics.

Polarity, as was said, is also a normative principle. As such it is primarily the principle of synthesis, of inclusiveness, of harmony, of cooperation. It is the mode of regarding other views, other policies, other individuals, or other groups as opposites rather than as opposed. Love, cooperation, inclusiveness are the guiding spirit here. Sheldon applies this principle to his metaphysics, ethics, and social problems. One could apply it to family relations, to educational, economic, and political activities; it could, in short, be applied to every form of activity. Certainly, a great deal can be said in favor of polarity as a normative principle, and Sheldon says it effectively and persuasively. Yet the polarity principle, like all other pervasive principles, has its limitations. There are situations, as in human relations for instance, where one should make more use of the principle of opposing, rather than of opposites. In dealing with moral evil there is a point where one should oppose it, fight it rather than try to assimilate it. It is true that in one sense synthesis, harmony, cooperation are higher principles, yet one must find a place in one's ethics for uncompromising opposition to evil, for righteous anger, for justified pugnacity. Probably Sheldon would accept this suggestion, for evil is not the opposite of good for him; yet if he does, then polarity should not be taken as *the* sole universal normative principle, as he seems to regard it.

4. *The Grades of Being*. While polarity gives balance, the grades of being mark the aspiration of being. Their basis is the principle of plenitude, which asserts a tendency in nature to realize all possibles.

Chance, from this standpoint, does not mean that anything may happen, but rather that in time everything must happen.

Being as realization of possibilities has degrees; and degrees of being are degrees of value. Degree is of the essence of value; so it is of being, but not "of being as just existence, only of being as existence realizing potencies; and potencies, essences, these are intrinsically greater or smaller".[34] And the scale of being is such that as it goes from the simplest to the most inclusive, each stage includes the power of the level next below, yet adds a contribution of its own that is not quite reducible to the terms of the other. God as the highest form of being is thus the highest good.

In this connection Sheldon presents an original version of the ontological argument for the existence of God.[35] Since, as he argues, a rational world is one in which all possibilities are equally realizable, then God must exist, for God is the realization of all possibilities in one act of being. In his own words, "If Anselm's 'idea of perfection' were understood as the sum total of all the ultimate possibles and if it were seen that the equal realization of all needs no explanation but is self-explaining, Anselm's proof would be sound".[36] Having established God's existence, we do not stand alone in our struggle for the good. And for Sheldon man's will is ultimately powerless for good without some assurance of God.

Sheldon's theory of the grades of being involves certain issues and difficulties. First, there is a possible alternative to Sheldon's conception that all possibilities are equally realizable. If one assumes that the determining conditions of actualities were from eternity, then all possibilities were not realizable but only those that were potential of actualities. Sheldon himself makes clear the distinction between pure possibilities and existential possibilities. In the realm of pure possibilities everything is possible; there are no incompatibles, all things are compossible. He even makes a case for round squares.[37] The only things that are not compatible are a proposition and its denial, but these are not two things in the sense of qualities, entities, relations, events, or terms. In the realm of existential possibilities

---

[34] *Ibid.*, p. 703.

[35] First stated in his article on "Another Form of the Ontological Proof", *Philosophical Review*, Vol. XXXII (1923), No. 4, pp. 355-372.

[36] *God and Polarity*, p. 527.

[37] *America's Progressive Philosophy*, pp. 169-170.

there are degrees of possibility : certain things are highly probable; others are possible under favorable conditions; still others are improbable or even impossible.

Secondly, even should one grant Sheldon's theory of absolute chance, it does not follow that the grades of being and God, as described by him, actually exist, but only that in time they must exist. The determination of what actually exists is an empirical question. It should also be noted that according to this theory the present mode of being as even God must eventually disappear, since in infinite time all possibilities will have to be realized.

What is of value in Sheldon's theory of the grades of being is his emphasis on the rich, qualitative, non-reductive aspect of existence. What is also of great value is his claim, in this connection, that "possibles make progress possible". This is true to the extent that human intelligence and action intervene to choose, control, and realize possibilities. All existent things have hidden possibilities, not merely unrealized possibilities but conflicting possibilities. Atomic energy has possibilities for human welfare as well as for human destruction; plants have possibilities for growth as well as for decay: human beings have possibilities for living in mutual respect and cooperation as well as for destroying one another. Progress means realizing more and more ideal possibilities.

5. *Synthesis.* This aspect of Sheldon's philosophy is in many respects the most important. His book, despite the author's genuine humility, urbanity, and generous spirit, is metaphysically one of the most ambitious undertakings. In terms of his principles of polarity and grades of being he attempts to formulate a synthetic philosophy that will increase one's insight into all major metaphysical systems; that will achieve an overall order in which some independence is allowed among members or phases of reality; that will end the strife of systems and provide a common basis for metaphysics. Has he succeeded in this enterprise?

First, it should be pointed out that a synthetic view need not inevitably be a truer view. If there are two possible interpretations of an issue, it does not necessairly follow that the synthetic one is truer than the other; either may be the actually true. In the case of conflict between two philosophic schools, it may be that one of the schools gives a truer account of reality than the other, and there is nothing to guarantee that a synthesis of their conflicting views would be more nearly true. Nevertheless it must be acknowledged that Sheldon is basically right in claiming that an adequate metaphysics must be synthetic in the sense that it must survey all phases of existence and do justice to all insights, an impartiality that can scarcely be expected of a partisan view.

One may admit the truth of Sheldon's major contention that one's philosophy ought to be synthetic. This emphasis is especially desirable at a time when philosophers, particularly in England and in this country, have been giving too much attention to the analytic phase of philosophy at the expense of its synthetic phase. Yet the question remains whether Sheldon's synthetic metaphysics is an adequate metaphysics, whether his philosophy is acceptable as a common basis for conflicting systems. How can one settle this issue?

In the past, synthetic systems were mostly deductive. Starting from certain allegedly self-evident principles, philosophic systems were built out of the implications of these principles. Adequacy meant that the premises were convincingly self-evident and the implications logical. In recent synthetic philosophies, such as Alexander's, Whitehead's, or Dewey's, this procedure has been increasingly rejected. They are more empirical and more descriptive. Sheldon's metaphysics is basically of this type, though he employs certain guiding principles. And for an empirical metaphysics the final test is not mere logical coherence, though this has its place, but rather the consideration whether the proposed synthetic pattern satisfactorily fits together the different aspects of experience, that is, impresses one with the substantial soundness of the system. On the basis of this test Sheldon's metaphysics is illuminating and highly adequate though not wholly, for many would find it difficult to assimilate within an empirical metaphysics his dualism and supernaturalism.

It is not a great misfortune, as Sheldon assumes, that we have, and probably will always have, a variety of philosophic systems. Ultimately individual experiences and decisions enter in, which are bound to emphasize one or another approach, one or another major outlook. This does not necessarily mean that we may not gradually move towards a common metaphysical system, but in the face of the infinite complexity and the mystery of existence we can at best offer varied, tentative systems. Yet enlightened action need not wait for a common synthetic philosophy. As long as basic agreements exist in the moral and political spheres, which is quite possible in spite of differences in metaphysical systems, we need not be hampered in common humane action.

Yet it must be admitted that, although his synthetic metaphysics may not end the strife of systems, Sheldon has basically succeeded in his great enterprise. He has made us aware of many of our unnecessary exclusive claims; he has also given us a magnificent metaphysical system, probably the most catholic one in contemporary philosophy, a system of great range and of many insights and values.

JOURNALS OF FIRST PUBLICATION

I. "Dewey and the Ethics of Naturalism", *The New Republic*, October 27, 1949.

II. "Cohen's Rationalistic Naturalism", *Philosophy and Phenomenological Research*, December, 1968.

III. "Singer's Philosophy of Experimentalism", *The Philosophy of Science*, January, 1962.

IV. "Hocking and the Dilemmas of Modernity", *The Journal of Philosophy*, March 27, 1958.

V. "The Philosophy of Alfred North Whitehead", Part I, *The New Republic*, August 6, 1951. Part II, *The Nation*, November 21, 1959.

VI. "Sheldon's Synthetic Metaphysics", *The Journal of Philosophy*, July, 1955.

INDEX